THE DEAD SEA SCROLLS

THE DEAD SEA SCROLLS
QUESTIONS AND RESPONSES FOR LATTER-DAY SAINTS

Donald W. Parry and Stephen D. Ricks

The Foundation for Ancient Research and Mormon Studies (FARMS)
at Brigham Young University
Provo, Utah

Donald W. Parry earned a Ph.D. in Hebrew literature and language from the University of Utah. He is associate professor of Hebrew language and literature in the Department of Asian and Near Eastern Languages at Brigham Young University. He is a member of the FARMS board of trustees.

Stephen D. Ricks earned a Ph.D. in Near Eastern religions from the University of California, Berkeley, and Graduate Theological Union. He is professor of Hebrew and cognate learning in the Department of Asian and Near Eastern Languages at Brigham Young University. He is a member of the FARMS board of trustees.

The Foundation for Ancient Research and Mormon Studies (FARMS)
at Brigham Young University
P.O. Box 7113
University Station
Provo, Utah 84602

Library of Congress Cataloging-in-Publication Data

Parry, Donald W.
    The Dead Sea scrolls : questions and responses for Latter-Day Saints /
Donald W. Parry and Stephen D. Ricks
        p. cm.
    Includes bibliographical references and index
    ISBN 0-934893-51-9
    1. Dead Sea scrolls—Introductions. I. Ricks, Stephen David. II. Title.

BM 487 .P34 2000
296.1'55—dc21
                                            00-0021497

CONTENTS

PART VIII: SPECIFIC INSIGHTS INTO THE DEAD SEA SCROLLS

ILLUSTRATIONS

PREFACE

What is the *Copper Scroll?* Do the Dead Sea Scrolls contain lost books of the Bible? Did John the Baptist study with the people of Qumran? What is the *Temple Scroll?* What about DNA research and the scrolls?

We have responded to scores of such questions on many occasions—while teaching graduate seminars and Hebrew courses at Brigham Young University, presenting papers at professional symposia, and speaking to various lay audiences. These settings are always positive experiences for us, particularly because they reveal that the general membership of the Church of Jesus Christ of Latter-day Saints has a deep interest in the scrolls and other writings from the ancient world.

The nonbiblical Dead Sea Scrolls are of great import because they shed much light on the cultural, religious, and political position of some of the Jews who lived shortly before and during the time of Jesus Christ. The biblical scrolls and the scrolls that have biblical themes are of even greater significance because they present valuable information regarding the ancient world and the way that the Old Testament was preserved, copied, and transmitted through the ages.

Latter-day Saints will recognize many truths in the scrolls. Even so, the scrolls should be approached with the same caution that the Lord revealed concerning those who read the Apocrypha: "There are many things contained therein that are true . . . ; there are many things contained therein that are not true. . . . Therefore, whoso readeth it, let him understand, for the Spirit manifesteth truth; . . . and whoso receiveth not by the Spirit, cannot be benefited" (Doctrine and Covenants 91:1–2, 4, 6).

This small volume, inspired by Joseph A. Fitzmyer's book *Responses to 101 Questions on the Dead Sea Scrolls,*[1] gathers information on seventy such questions into a single work. While many of the questions we respond to are ones that Latter-day Saints have asked us, we also selected questions that will be of further interest to them. We added still more questions in order to balance our goal of addressing Latter-day Saints with the need for adequate coverage of the scrolls in general. In any case, because we wrote this book with an LDS audience foremost in mind, many of our responses treat themes of particular interest to Latter-day Saints (e.g., baptism, prophecy, premortal life, and the plan of salvation), include LDS terminology, and refer to LDS scripture.

Our brief volume does not attempt to touch upon all aspects of the Dead Sea Scrolls, nor does it attempt to be comprehensive in its treatment of selected topics. Rather, we have prepared this book with the needs of the general reader foremost in mind. We have included various illustrations so that the reader can visualize the scrolls, the caves where they were discovered, and the ruins of Qumran, among other points of interest. Because we have kept endnote citations to a minimum, readers desiring additional information on the scrolls are encouraged to consult the select bibliography found in the final response of this book.

Our preparation of this volume does not imply a historical or theological connection between the beliefs of the people of Qumran and Latter-day Saints. Numerous similarities exist between any two religious groups, but there are also differences—and the differences often are more consequential than the similarities. While we may see several similarities between Latter-day Saints and the writers of the Dead Sea Scrolls, we also see equally interesting similarities between the latter group and religious groups of other historical periods and locales. There are actually far more differences between the Qumranites and the Latter-day Saints than there are similarities.

We have tried to avoid subjects of scholarly controversy. For instance, we do not attempt to settle the issue of who—Essenes, Sadducees, another Jewish group?—owned or possessed the scrolls and later hid them in the caves near Qumran. We have also tried to avoid the sensationalism and gratuitous comparisons between Latter-day Saints and the Qumran people that have marred many publications and public presentations on the scrolls. The Dead Sea Scrolls are sensational enough without such embellishments; they stand on their own as being the greatest manuscript discovery of the twentieth century.

With few exceptions, we have used the translation of the Dead Sea Scrolls by Geza Vermes, *The Complete Dead Sea Scrolls in English* (New York: Penguin, 1997), which is responsibly prepared, accepted by the scholarly community, and readily available in libraries and bookstores. Scroll translations included in our book were drawn from Vermes's work unless otherwise noted.

We would like to thank the many people who have so ably assisted us in preparing this volume. Jeanette Miller helped us with research and work on early drafts of some of the responses. Gaye Strathearn and Dana M. Pike of the Department of Ancient Scripture at Brigham Young University and Alison V. P. Coutts of the Foundation for Ancient Research and Mormon Studies at BYU reviewed the early manuscript and offered helpful comments. We also thank Don L. Brugger of FARMS for his careful and sensitive editing and for his very considerable insight in guiding the book through to completion. Other FARMS associates competently performed additional tasks: Whitney Fox and K. Laura Sommer checked the sources; Stephanie Christensen, Alison V. P. Coutts, Paula W. Hicken, and Sandra A. Thorne proofread the edited manuscript; and Mary Mahan designed and typeset the book. The cover concept and design are the commendable work of J. Scott Knudsen. To all of these we express our heartfelt thanks.

PART I

DESCRIPTION, DISCOVERY, AND DISPOSITION OF THE DEAD SEA SCROLLS

1. What are the Dead Sea Scrolls?

The Dead Sea Scrolls comprise a collection of several hundred texts discovered between the years 1947 and 1956 in eleven caves near the northwest shore of the Dead Sea. These scrolls are believed to have belonged to a Jewish community of Essenes (see questions 6 and 67) who lived in nearby Qumran (see question 4). However, numerous texts discovered in other locations in the Judean desert, such as Wadi Murabbaʿat, Masada, Nahal Hever, Khirbet Mird, Nahal Mishmar, and Wadi ed-Daliyeh, are also called Dead Sea Scrolls.

The great majority of scrolls are written in Hebrew on animal skins or papyrus. The scrolls form a significant body of literature, both secular and religious, that originated during the Second Temple period of Judaism (about 250 B.C.–A.D. 70). Unfortunately, most of the scrolls are fragmentary, having been damaged over the centuries by the natural elements and, as it appears in some cases, by individuals who trampled them underfoot.

2. How were the scrolls discovered?

In 1947 (some accounts say 1945) Muhammad ed-Dhib ("Muhammad the Wolf"), a young Arab boy of the Taʿamireh Bedouin tribe, was walking in the hills northwest of the Dead Sea, possibly in search of a stray goat, when he discovered a small cave opening and tossed small stones inside. The first stone struck something and made a plinking sound; the second stone resulted in a crash that sent the boy scurrying down the hill in terror of *jinn*, local spirits that were said to inhabit waste places in the wilderness.

The following day Muhammad, regaining his courage and returning with a companion, possibly his cousin Muhammad Jumʿa, succeeded in penetrating the tiny opening to the cave now known as Cave 1. There he discovered a cache of clay jars, some of which contained several scrolls in a near-perfect state of preservation. He returned with several scrolls that were eventually passed on, through middlemen, to scholars who identified the scrolls as Jewish and dating to around the time of Christ. In more recent years, Muhammad ed-Dhib, who lived in Bethlehem until his recent death, stated that he was searching for hidden treasure, not looking for lost goats, and that it may not have been 1947, but perhaps months, even a year or two, earlier when he made his initial discovery of the scrolls.[2]

3. Where were the scrolls discovered?

The Dead Sea Scrolls were discovered in eleven caves north and south of an ancient site called Qumran. Besides the manuscripts discovered in Cave 1, ancient writings were discovered in ten additional caves in subsequent years. Archaeologists were responsible for finding two of these caves (Caves 3 and 5), workmen at the Qumran site found four more (Caves 7, 8, 9, and 10), and the Taʿamireh tribesmen, who according to

Dead Sea Scrolls scholar Geza Vermes often "succeeded in out-witting their professional rivals,"[3] discovered Caves 2, 4, 6, and 11. Since 1947 other texts and documents dating from the same era as the Dead Sea Scrolls (250 B.C.–A.D. 70) have been found in other locations near the Dead Sea, including Wadi Murabbaʿat, Masada, Nahal Hever, Khirbet Mird, Nahal Mishmar, and Wadi ed-Daliyeh.

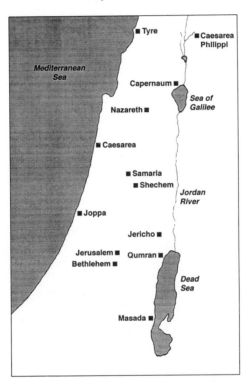

The Holy Land, showing Qumran located near the northwest shore of the Dead Sea. Map by Jeff Jolley.

4. What is Qumran?

Qumran is the Arabic name for the area including Wadi Qumran and Khirbet Qumran, located one kilometer inland from the northwestern side of the Dead Sea. (The term *wādī* is Arabic for a "[dried-up] river bed"; *khirba/beh/bet* is Arabic for a "[site of] ruins.")[4] Wadi Qumran runs to the south of a high plateau on which is located Khirbet Qumran. Some of the caves are located along cliffs on the north side of the wadi at the southern edge of Khirbet Qumran, while others are found about a kilometer north of Khirbet Qumran.

Different theories concerning Khirbet Qumran's original use have been proposed. Before Roland de Vaux excavated the site of Khirbet Qumran in 1951, the generally accepted view

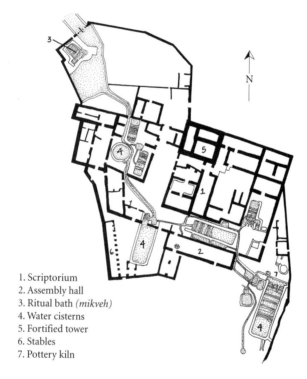

1. Scriptorium
2. Assembly hall
3. Ritual bath *(mikveh)*
4. Water cisterns
5. Fortified tower
6. Stables
7. Pottery kiln

Diagram of Qumran based on the excavation. The building complex was probably built around 140 B.C. and inhabited until A.D. 68, when the community was apparently dispersed or destroyed by Roman soldiers. Drawing by Michael P. Lyon.

was that it had been an old Roman fortress.[5] The most widely accepted theory today, one proposed by de Vaux, is that the central building was used as a community center for a Jewish religious group. In the building complex, places have been found for dining, ritual washing, and the transcribing of scrolls.[6]

According to most scholars, the inhabitants of Qumran probably did not dwell in the complex of buildings but, rather, resided in nearby caves, as evidenced by more than two dozen caves examined by archaeologists and found to contain signs of habitation.

The size of the cemetery located near the ruins and other archaeological evidence indicate that the community at Qumran may have numbered from 150 to 300 individuals at any one time. The building complex there appears to have first been built about 140 B.C., and its final destruction dates to about A.D. 68.[7] In 140 B.C., when the community settled at Qumran, the building complex was much smaller in size. However, some decades later the complex was enlarged, and the community continued to grow until 31 B.C. The historian Josephus recorded that there was a large earthquake in Palestine at that time, and archaeological evidence shows that an earthquake and fire caused the first destruction of the community. There is some debate about when the area was reoccupied, but the latest date was probably around 4 B.C.

5. What types of texts were discovered among the scrolls?

The scrolls, most of which are fragmentary, belong to a variety of text types, including the following:

1. Books of the Hebrew Bible (the Christian Old Testament). These books include Genesis, Exodus, 1 and 2 Samuel, Isaiah, and Malachi, to name a few. The fragmentary remains of every book of the Hebrew Bible except the book of Esther have been discovered among the scrolls.

2. Aramaic translations of the Hebrew Bible. Aramaic is a Northwest Semitic language similar to Hebrew. In the centuries before and shortly after the ministry of Christ, many Jews used Aramaic as their primary language. Jews translated the Old Testament from Hebrew into Aramaic so they could continue to read and study it. Parts of the books of Job, Leviticus, and other biblical books written in Aramaic have been discovered among the scrolls.

3. Tephillin and Mezuzot. Tephillin (singular *tephillah*), also called phylacteries (see Matthew 23:5), are small boxes (made of a variety of woods or metals) attached to cords that are bound to the head and left arm. Within the boxes are very small parchments containing verses from the books of Exodus and Deuteronomy (usually including Exodus 13:1–16 and Deuteronomy 6:4–6; 11:13–21). The idea of *tephillin* originated from Deuteronomy 6:8: "Thou shalt bind them [certain words of the Lord] for a sign upon thine hand, and they shall be as frontlets between thine eyes." Even today the *tephillin* are used by orthodox Jews during prayers. Approximately thirty *tephillin* texts have been found in the Qumran caves.

Mezuzot (singular *mezuzah*) are small boxes or containers attached to the right side of the doorpost of a house. Each box contains a parchment with passages from Deuteronomy (usually Deuteronomy 6:4–6 and 11:13–21). The tradition of *mezuzot* arose from the command in Deuteronomy 6:9: "Thou shalt write them upon the posts of thy house, and on thy gates." The caves of Qumran have yielded eight *mezuzot* texts.

4. Biblical commentaries. Several scrolls comprise commentaries that explain books in the Old Testament. Commentaries on the books of Psalms, Isaiah, Hosea, Micah, Nahum, Habakkuk, Zephaniah, and Malachi have been discovered among the scrolls.

5. *Apocryphal writings.* The term *apocrypha* originally meant "hidden" or "secret" and pertains to religious books that, for a number of reasons, were not included in the Hebrew Bible.[8] Several apocryphal books have been discovered among the Dead Sea Scrolls, including Tobit, Sirach (also called Ecclesiasticus), and Letter of Jeremiah.

Doctrine and Covenants 91:1–2 provides guidelines on how to approach apocryphal writings. The statement concerns *the* Apocrypha (i.e., those books found in the Catholic Old Testament—such as Judith, 1 and 2 Maccabees, Susanna, and Bel and the Dragon—that are not in the Protestant Old Testament): "Verily, thus saith the Lord unto you concerning the Apocrypha—There are many things contained therein that are true, and it is mostly translated correctly; there are many things contained therein that are not true, which are interpolations by the hands of men."

6. *Pseudepigraphic writings.* The term *pseudepigrapha* is a Greek term meaning "falsely attributed writings," or writings of questionable authorship that purport to be written by certain biblical heroes and prophets (such as Enoch, Noah, Isaiah, Abraham, Isaac, and Joseph). These writings, popular among the Qumran people and other Jews of their day, present concepts regarding the prophetic, historical, political, cultural, and religious status of institutions of the period. Pseudepigraphic writings found among the scrolls include the *Book of Enoch,* the *Book of Noah,* the *Testament of Amram,* the *Samuel Apocryphon, Second Ezekiel, Para-Danielic Writings, Jubilees, Pseudo-Moses,* and the *Testament of Levi.*

7. *Writings for worship.* Many texts concern the worship practices of the Qumran people, providing information about prayers, blessings, hymns, and rituals. These texts are called *Benedictions, Purification Ritual, Prayer or Hymn Celebrating*

the *Morning and the Evening, Thanksgiving Hymns, Daily Prayers, Blessings, Prayers for Festivals*, and *Bless, My Soul*. Unfortunately, most of the texts are incomplete, as only scroll fragments remain.

8. Legal documents. The Qumran caves yielded a number of religious legal texts that describe rules and regulations belonging to the Qumran community. These texts include the *Damascus Document*, the *Community Rule*, the *Temple Scroll*, and *Some Observances of the Law* (also known as *4QMMT*).

9. Business records. Few in number, business records among the scrolls reveal accounts of money and grain, the sale of property, and records pertaining to debt.

10. The Copper Scroll. This unique text contains a record of supposed treasures that were hidden in various locations throughout ancient Palestine.

11. Writings focusing on the last days. Describing events associated with the end of time, these religious texts are titled the *War Scroll, Words of the Archangel Michael,* and the *New Jerusalem*.

12. Poetic compositions and wisdom literature. Many poems pertaining to the study and obtaining of wisdom were discovered among the scrolls, including *The Seductress, Exhortation to Seek Wisdom, Parable of the Tree, Beatitudes, Noncanonical Psalms, Thanksgiving Hymns,* and *Lamentations*.

13. Calendrical texts. These writings deal with the calendar used by the Qumran people. They are named *Phases of the Moon, Calendars of Priestly Courses, Calendric Signs,* and *Horoscopes or Astrological Physiognomies*.

6. Who wrote or possessed the Qumran texts?

Josephus, a first-century-a.d. Jewish military leader and historian, describes a variety of Jewish groups who were active in the last centuries B.C. and the first centuries A.D., including the Boethusians, Essenes, Pharisees, Sadducees, and Zealots. From contemporary and near-contemporary accounts of the beliefs and practices of these communities, scholars have noted similarities between descriptions of these groups and the writings in the Dead Sea Scrolls. Two groups in particular have received attention in this regard: the Sadducees and the Essenes.

A few scholars believe that the writers of the Dead Sea Scrolls were Sadducees or proto-Sadduccees. This judgment is based mostly on material found in a document among the scrolls now known as *Some Observances of the Law (4QMMT)*. However, other scholars have noted that the points of comparison are not particularly strong.[9]

Most scholars agree that the writers and owners of the scrolls were Essenes. This conclusion is based on comparing the scrolls with statements made by Josephus and others. Dead Sea Scrolls scholar Todd Beall recently published a book that takes this approach. Although he found in the writings of Josephus six statements about the Essenes that are apparently at odds with ideas in the Qumran scrolls, he also found twenty-six other statements by Josephus that are parallel to Qumranite beliefs and practices.[10] For example, Josephus made the following observations concerning the Essenes:[11]

1. They must be Jews by birth.
2. They "despise riches and their sharing of goods is admirable; there is not found among them any one who has greater wealth than another. For it is a law that those entering the group transfer their property to the order; consequently, among them all there appears neither abject poverty nor superabundance of wealth, but the possessions of each are mingled together, and there is, as among brothers, one property common to all."[12]

3. They replace neither clothing nor sandals.
4. They avoid spitting.
5. They always dress in white.

All five of these statements accord with similar statements set forth in the Qumran sectarian writings.

Furthermore, Pliny the Elder, a Roman scholar and scientist, made the following statement regarding the Essenes:

> To the west [of the Dead Sea] the Essenes have put the necessary distance between themselves and the insalubrious shore. They are a people unique of its kind and admirable beyond all others in the whole world without women and renouncing love entirely, without money, and having for company only the palm trees. Owing to the throng of newcomers, this people is daily re-born in equal number; indeed, those whom, wearied by the fluctuations of fortune, life leads to adopt their customs, stream in in great numbers. Thus, unbelievable though this may seem, for thousands of centuries a race has existed which is eternal yet into which no one is born: so fruitful for them is the repentance which others feel for their past lives![13]

Although this brief passage by Pliny contains some factual or historical errors, its details about the Essenes parallel ideas found in the scrolls: renouncing money, experiencing an increase in converts, and the long existence of the group. Also, Pliny's statement places the Essenes' geographical location at or near Qumran. However, Pliny's comments can still be interpreted in more than one way, making positive identification of the inhabitants of Qumran nearly impossible.

7. When were the scrolls written or copied?

Scholars generally agree that the scrolls were written or copied between the years 250 B.C. and A.D. 70. This calculation is based on four scientific methods:

1. Paleographic analysis. Paleography is the science of deciphering ancient writing styles. After a careful examination of the way that the scrolls' Hebrew characters were written by the scribes, Professor Frank Moore Cross of Harvard University placed the scrolls in three time periods: the Archaic period (250–150 B.C.), the Hasmonean period (150–30 B.C.), and the Herodian period (30 B.C.–A.D. 68/70).[14]

2. Accelerator Mass Spectrometry (AMS). This method of dating the scrolls is similar to the carbon-14 dating system. Of the eight scrolls tested by AMS, seven agree generally with their paleographic dating.[15]

3. Archaeological discoveries. Archaeologists have found pottery and coins in many of the caves in which the scrolls were found. The pottery and coins can often be dated to a specific time period.

4. Historical allusions. On rare occasions the scrolls allude to events or characters of known dates in the historical record.

8. Why are the scrolls so important?

The scrolls have been called the most important manuscript find of this century because they have greatly increased our knowledge of the Hebrew Bible, Second Temple Judaism (450 B.C.–A.D. 70), the Hebrew language, and various religious texts. The scrolls have attracted so much attention that more than seven thousand books, articles, dissertations, and other writings, as well as television documentaries and news stories, have focused on them. Also, new academic journals have appeared that are dedicated to the study of the scrolls, and participants in professional conferences discuss their value.

The scrolls significantly enhance scholarly research in many areas, including the following:

1. Ancient writing and scribal practices
2. How words were spelled anciently
3. Different handwriting styles
4. Old Testament studies, including the history and transmission of the biblical text and variant readings in the text
5. The making of ancient scrolls from leather or papyrus
6. Linguistic studies in the languages of Hebrew and Aramaic
7. Apocryphal and pseudepigraphic studies
8. Religious groups and their ideas within Palestinian Judaism
9. Ancient methods of biblical interpretation
10. The history of Jewish groups from 250 B.C. to A.D. 70
11. Background studies of the pre-Christian era

9. In what language were the scrolls written?

The majority of the scrolls, biblical and nonbiblical, were written in Hebrew, the language of the ancient Israelites and the sacred language of the Jews.

Alphabets in paleo-Hebrew (Old Hebrew), in Qumran Hebrew (from the *Great Isaiah Scroll*), and in Roman characters.

A few of the scrolls, including the book of Daniel, the apocryphal book of Tobit, fragments of the books of Job and Leviticus, the *Genesis Apocryphon,* the *Book of Enoch,* and the *Testament of Levi* were written in Aramaic. Aramaic is a sister language to Hebrew, sharing with it the same alphabet and numerous grammatical features. A few scroll manuscripts of the Old Testament were written in Greek.

10. How many caves have yielded scrolls?

Eleven caves located near Qumran have yielded scrolls or scroll fragments. For convenience, scholars call these caves, in order of their discovery, Cave 1, Cave 2, Cave 3, Cave 4, and so on. Since 1956 no additional caves have yielded more than a few small fragments of scrolls.

Cave 1, located about one mile north of the Qumran ruins, was the first of the eleven caves to yield scrolls. The seven major scrolls of Cave 1 are the *Community Rule, Rule of the Congregation,* the *War Scroll,* the *Thanksgiving Hymns,* the *Genesis Apocryphon, Commentary on Habakkuk,* and the *Great Isaiah Scroll.* Cave 2, located near Cave 1, was discovered by Bedouins in February 1952. It yielded eighteen fragmentary Old Testament texts and fifteen nonbiblical texts, including a text about the New Jerusalem and two copies of *Jubilees.*

Archaeologists discovered Cave 3, which yielded fourteen fragmentary texts, three of them biblical and eleven nonbiblical. Cave 3 also contained the *Copper Scroll,* a twelve-column text inscribed on copper sheets that describes the location of presumed temple treasures containing massive amounts of gold, silver, and precious objects.

Cave 4, discovered in 1952, is an "artificially hewn cave" with "regularly spaced rows of holes found in the cave's walls."[16] The manuscripts found there are among the most significant of the Dead Sea Scrolls discoveries. Scholars estimate that between 500 and 600 different texts, all fragmented, were found in Cave 4. Of these, approximately 130 are biblical texts and the remainder are nonbiblical, including fragments of the

Community Rule, the *Damascus Document,* the *Testament of Levi,* and *Jubilees.*

When archaeologists discovered Cave 5 in September 1952, it yielded eight biblical and seventeen nonbiblical texts, including fragments of the *Community Rule,* the *Damascus Document,* and an Aramaic text concerning the New Jerusalem.

Cave 6, which was located by Taʿamireh Bedouin, yielded seven biblical and more than twenty nonbiblical texts, including fragments from the books of Genesis and Leviticus, which were written in an archaic Hebrew script called paleo-Hebrew.

Archaeologists discovered Cave 7 in 1955 and recovered nineteen tiny Greek fragments, two of which have been identified as Exodus 28:4–7 and Baruch 6:43–44. The remaining fragments are too small to decipher.

During the months of February and March in 1955, archaeologists discovered Caves 7 through 10. Cave 8 yielded four biblical fragments, a phylactery, a *mezuzah,* and a hymnic text. Cave 9 held only a small papyrus with six Hebrew characters, and Cave 10 yielded a potsherd containing written inscriptions.

In January 1956 the Bedouin found Cave 11, which yielded the famous *Temple Scroll,* the longest of the Dead Sea Scrolls, measuring approximately eight meters long. Other finds in Cave 11 include the *Apocryphal Psalms,* which contain many psalms from the biblical book of Psalms and seven other psalms not found in our Bible, a fragmentary copy of Leviticus written in paleo-Hebrew, and fragments of the books of Deuteronomy and Ezekiel. In addition, Cave 11 contained fragments of texts from the books of *Jubilees, The Heavenly Prince Melchizedek,* the *Targum of Job,* and *Songs for the Holocaust of the Sabbath Sacrifice.*

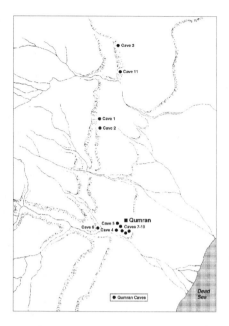

The eleven caves near Qumran yielded the fragmentary remains of more than eight hundred biblical and nonbiblical writings dating from about 300 B.C.

11. How were the scrolls stored in the caves?

The scrolls of Cave 1 were found intact, wrapped in linen, stored in jars, and sealed in a nearly inaccessible location. They appear to have been prepared for storage more carefully than the other scrolls were. The Cave 1 scrolls may have constituted part of the library at Qumran, and the difficult access to the cave suggests that it was used as a hiding place for the scrolls.

The scrolls found in the other caves seem to have been placed there very hastily, without protection against the elements. The Cave 4 scrolls, for instance, were found among centuries of accumulated debris that, at the time of their discovery, reached a height of nearly three feet. As a result, the Cave 4 scrolls exist only in fragmentary condition.

12. Have there been scroll discoveries in recent years?

Since 1956 there have been no significant scroll discoveries, although many people have searched the Dead Sea coastline and the Judean hills in the hope of finding more scrolls and other artifacts. Israeli archaeologists Magen Broshi and Hanan Eshel, for example, led an expedition to the Qumran area in 1995 and 1996 and examined seven caves located in the plateau northwest of the Qumran ruins. They found hundreds of pottery shards from jars, dishes, and jugs and concluded that some of the caves served as residences for members of the Qumran community. No scrolls were recovered from the seven caves.[17]

13. What is the value of the scrolls?

Once it was determined that the scrolls and fragments were of great monetary value, many were purchased and then resold at higher prices. Antiquities dealers, collectors, museums, and universities played various roles in the acquisition of the scrolls. Some transactions were for profit, while others resulted in the acquisition of scrolls by universities for academic study and publication. The following *Wall Street Journal* advertisement, dated 1 June 1954, illustrates the manner in which the scrolls were treated by dealers shortly after their discovery.

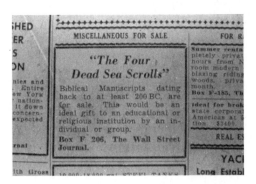

Despite the buying and selling of the scrolls during the early years subsequent to their discovery, today, fortunately for the world community, most of the scrolls are in museums where they are stored in climate-controlled depositories or displayed for viewing.

14. Where are the scrolls stored now?

Most of the scrolls are presently housed in two museums in Jerusalem. The seven major scrolls from Cave 1 are located in the Shrine of the Book, part of the Israel Museum. The Shrine of the Book is unique because its roof resembles the shape of an earthenware lid, similar to the lids that were on the jars of Cave 1. The inside of the building is underground, designed to resemble the interior of a cave. Displayed within this museum are numerous scrolls and scroll fragments of the Dead Sea Scrolls, including a high-quality facsimile of the *Great Isaiah Scroll.*

The Shrine of the Book in Jerusalem, the museum in which the seven original scrolls from Cave 1 are kept. Photograph courtesy of Stephen W. Booras.

Thousands of scroll pieces and fragments from Caves 1, 4, and 11 are found in the "scrollery" of the Rockefeller Museum (formerly called the Palestine Archaeological Museum), located in East Jerusalem. These have been photographed and set in humidity-controlled areas under protective plates of glass. The *Copper Scroll* from Cave 3 and a number of fragments from Cave 1 are located at the Museum of the Department of Antiquities in Amman, Jordan.

The Rockefeller Museum in Jerusalem houses thousands of scroll fragments. Photograph courtesy of David Harris, Jerusalem.

15. What is the state of preservation of the scrolls?

The state of preservation of the scrolls varies considerably. Although eleven nearly complete manuscripts of the Dead Sea Scrolls have been discovered, fragments of several hundred other scrolls are in various stages of deterioration, some the size of a postage stamp or smaller.

Scholars believe that the scrolls of Cave 4 were once stored on wooden shelves that eventually rotted, split, and collapsed, leaving the scrolls for centuries exposed to the moisture, dirt, insects, and worms on the cave floor. Almost two thousand years later, when the Bedouins discovered the cave, they found the thousands of scroll fragments buried in debris.

Frank Moore Cross, a Harvard University professor emeritus and one of the first translators of the scrolls, describes his experience with the scrolls:

> On arrival at the Palestine Museum, purchased groups of fragments were in unbelievable disorder. Many large, well-preserved fragments came in each lot. But large or small, well or ill preserved, most had to be exposed to a process of humidification, cleaned of incrustations and dirt, and repaired or reinforced before being pressed flat between glass plates. Fragments in advanced decay, especially lumps of coagulated layers of leather, require more energy and patience and special techniques, though the same general procedure is followed. Often a fragment will exhibit an area of acute decay and shrinkage in the midst of otherwise pliable leather. The bad spot may draw the entire fragment into a crinkled or scalloped ball, so that the fragment is almost impossible to flatten. The script in such an area of decay may be shrunk to half or less the size of that in good areas. Often such decomposition in sheets of leather has caused splitting and fragmentation, and the problems of fitting into one manuscript healthy, light fragments alongside of wizened and blackened scraps are, to say the least, tedious.[18]

Many of the scrolls in Cave 1, in contrast to those described above from Cave 4, were found in a much better state of preservation because they were wrapped in cloth and then stored in jars. The *Copper Scroll* of Cave 3 was also fairly well preserved because of its metal content.

PART II

THE WRITERS OF THE
DEAD SEA SCROLLS

16. What happened to the writers of the scrolls?

The first century A.D. was a troubled period in Jewish history. After several unsuccessful regional uprisings, the entire population of Jerusalem and Judea revolted against Roman rule in A.D. 66. Vespasian (later to become Roman emperor from A.D. 71 to 78) was ordered to suppress the revolt. By A.D. 70 Rome had crushed the revolt in Judea and Galilee, Jerusalem lay in the grasp of its hated enemy, and the temple at Jerusalem was destroyed.

Things were not much safer for the community that owned the scrolls. Probably expecting that their community would shortly be dispersed, and wishing to prevent their writings from being seized or destroyed, members hid the scrolls in caves about A.D. 68–70 (scores of coins have been found in the Qumran caves that assist archaeologists in dating the ruins to this time period). Fire and the Roman attack destroyed the building complex, as evidenced by a number of Roman arrowheads that excavation has uncovered.[19] It is not known whether the inhabitants of the community were able to flee or whether they were killed or taken captive at that time.

The ruins of Qumran were excavated and partially restored between 1951 and 1956. Photograph courtesy of Melvin J. Thorne.

17. Why did the people of Qumran separate themselves from Jerusalem?

Scholars believe that the people of Qumran departed from Jerusalem or other parts of Israel to retreat from those who they believed were wicked or ritually impure. Members of the Qumran community believed that a very high degree of religious purity was necessary in order to be prepared for the end of times.

A legal document among the scrolls called *Some Observances of the Law (4QMMT)* lists differences between the Qumran group and other religious Jews, perhaps including those of Jerusalem. The document explains that there were at least twenty points of the law of Moses wherein the Jewish groups differed, including their respective views on the offering of sacrifices from the Gentiles, bringing certain animal skins to the temple, sacrificing pregnant animals, eating unborn animals, bringing dogs into Jerusalem, the marriage of priests, and items concerning lepers, the blind, and the deaf (see question 55). The text also explains that, as a result of different doctrinal interpretations, the Qumran people "have separated from the mass of the peo[ple] . . . and from mingling" in matters pertaining to religious uncleanness and impurity (*Some Observances of the Law* 7:7–11).

18. What was the Qumran community's view of the inspired interpretation of prophecy?

Qumran texts illustrate the belief in the inspired interpretation of scripture by one Jewish group that believed it was living in the last days, during which that gift had been renewed. The community as a whole was convinced that the Spirit of God, a gift for the last days, was present and active in their midst. Although the Holy Spirit is primarily regarded as the spirit of prophecy in Rabbinic Judaism, in Qumran the Holy Spirit has a function that is more broadly conceived in terms of cleansing, truth, holiness, and divinely mediated knowledge and insight. Apart from inspired interpretation of scripture, prophecy (as direct revelation mediated through inspired speech or writing) does not appear to have been practiced by the Teacher of Righteousness (see question 21) or other members of the Qumran community. For the Qumran community, inspired interpretation played a role equivalent to prophecy, yet it is readily apparent that the differences between the two phenomena are not small.[20]

19. Did the Qumran people believe they were living in the last days?

The writers of the Dead Sea Scrolls believed they were living in the last days. They considered themselves to be living in the end of times and preparing for the temple of the last days,[21] and they believed that the establishment of their community constituted the period "which will end with the final judgment."[22] They read and interpreted the scriptures in this light, likening the prophecies concerning the last days to themselves.

According to Frank Moore Cross, the Qumranites represented a group who lived "in anticipation of the Kingdom of God."[23] They anxiously looked forward to the coming of the Messiah, who they believed would cleanse the world and redeem them. The writers of the Qumran community's texts considered themselves to be not only the "remnant of Israel" of their time but also the "remnant" of all time, the final "remnant."

The *War Scroll* preserves an account of battles of the last days between the forces of righteousness, called the Sons of Light (under the direction of the Prince of Light), and the forces of evil, called the Sons of Darkness (under the direction of Belial). The latter forces, which were identified with "the traditional enemies of the Jewish people,"[24] would be annihilated for eternity.

20. Did the owners of the scrolls believe they were a covenant people?

In a very real sense, the owners of the Dead Sea Scrolls believed they were a covenant people—the "sons of light" (*Community Rule* 1:9; 2:16; *War Scroll* 1:1, 3, 9, 11, 13)—involved in a mortal struggle with the "sons of darkness" (*Community Rule* 1:10; *War Scroll* 1:1, 7, 10, 16). Becoming a member of the community involved entering into a "Covenant of Grace . . .

that they may be joined to the counsel of God and may live perfectly before Him in accordance with all that has been revealed" (*Community Rule* 1:7). The *Community Rule* contains some forty-five occurrences of the word *covenant,* while the *Damascus Document* contains forty-two.

21. Who are the "Teacher of Righteousness" and the "Wicked Priest"?

The scrolls identify the Teacher of Righteousness (Hebrew *moreh ha-tsedeq*) as a priest who appears to have been highly influential in the early history of the Qumran community. For reasons that remain unclear, the writers of the scrolls used code names instead of given names; thus the actual names of the Teacher of Righteousness and Wicked Priest can only be surmised. The appearance of the Teacher of Righteousness and his conflict with the Wicked Priest is a chapter in the wider history of the struggle between Hellenization and traditional Judaism.

The Hellenizers, who wanted Judaism to adopt Greek culture and values, were led by the family of Tobias. The traditionalists, who preferred to maintain the received values of Judaism and who viewed Greek influence as baneful, if not deadly, to Jewish life, were led by Onias III, a Zadokite[25] and the legitimate high priest, who is described as a "zealot for the laws" (2 Maccabees 4:2). The struggle between the Hellenizers and traditionalists became so intense that it threatened to break out in a full-scale civil war. Fearing such a turn of events, Onias went to Syria to plead the cause of the traditionalists and to affirm his support for Seleucus Philopator, the Syrian Greek ruler over Palestine (187 B.C.).[26] When Seleucus Philopator was assassinated in 176 B.C., he was succeeded by Antiochus IV (Epiphanes), who was not well-disposed toward Onias. In the view of some scholars, while in Syria Onias came into contact with members of the Dead Sea Scrolls community and became one of their guiding lights (possibly the Teacher of Righteousness) and was responsible for composing several texts of the Dead Sea Scrolls. Onias was deposed from his high priestly office by his brother Jason and, hearing of a plot against him, fled to Egypt. He was murdered in 172 B.C. on the orders of Menelaus, whom many Dead Sea Scrolls scholars regard as the Wicked Priest.

Although the Teacher of Righteousness did not refer to himself as "prophet," in many ways he functioned as one. For example, the *Commentary on Habbakuk* indicates that he provided inspired interpretation of scripture and was taught by God himself, who had poured out His spirit upon him (see 2:2–3; 7:4–7). In the Qumran scrolls, prophecy was related to the interpretation of scripture and to the community's concern with the last days:

> God told Habakkuk to write down that which would happen to the final generation, but He did not make known to him when time would come to an end. And as for that which He said, *That he who reads may read it speedily:* interpreted this concerns the Teacher of Righteousness, to whom God made known all the mysteries of the words of His servants the Prophets. (*Commentary on Habakuk* 7:1–5)

22. Were the ritual immersions at Qumran considered to be baptisms?

It is difficult to tell the significance of ritual immersions among Jews in antiquity, let alone try to determine the Qumran community's exact understanding of the practice from their writings. Archaeological evidence indicates that these immersions took place in a water installation (a type of font) called a *miqveh*. Scholars have seen the connections with Christian baptisms, observing "close contacts in language and thought between the early church and the Qumran community. Jesus was baptized by John the Baptist in the Jordan during the time when the community of covenanters was flourishing not many miles away. . . . [John's mode of baptizing] may have had some historical connection with the ritual bathing of the Qumran sect."[27]

The *Community Rule* states that purificatory immersions occur following a year of probation (see 3:4–6; 5:13–15). However, as Lawrence Schiffman notes, "to the sectarians, ritual purification was not more than a symptom of spiritual purification. Indeed, the sect believed that no amount of lustration or ablution would render pure anyone who was still an unrepentant transgressor."[28] This view is reflected in the *Community Rule:*

> He will not be purified by atonement rituals, nor will he become pure in waters of lustration.
> He will not be sanctified in seas or rivers,
> nor will he be purified in any waters of ablution.
> Impure, impure, he will remain as long as he despises the divine regulations, so as not
> to be disciplined by the counsel of His community. (3:4–6)[29]

PART III

TRANSLATION AND PUBLICATION INFORMATION

23. Who pieces together the scroll fragments?

Soon after the discovery of the scrolls, translators and scholars Roland de Vaux, Josef T. Milik, and Maurice Baillet began the process of sorting through the thousands of scroll fragments. Their goal was to piece together as many of the fragments as possible. The task was so large that other scholars were invited to help, including John M. Allegro, assistant lecturer at the University of Manchester; Frank Moore Cross, then a professor at McCormick Theological Seminary and annual professor at the American School of Oriental Research in Jerusalem; Patrick W. Skehan, a professor at the Catholic University of America; John Strugnell of Jesus College, Oxford; and Jean Starcky and Claus-Hunno Hunzinger. While most of the sorting and piecing of the scroll fragments was completed in the 1950s, some fifty years after the first discovery of scrolls in Cave 1, approximately sixty scholars are involved in sorting, editing, and translating the fragments.

24. How are the scroll fragments pieced together?

Most of the scrolls are very fragmentary—there are thousands of pieces of leather, parchment, or papyrus in various sizes and shapes. Because of the enormous challenge of sorting and piecing the fragments together, the scholars working on the scrolls developed the following approaches to help them determine which fragments belong to a specific text:

1. *Types of materials.* The fragments are first sorted into groups of leather parchment or papyri. Then the thickness and the color of the leather of each fragment are evaluated, thus continuing the sorting process.

2. *Scribal handwriting styles.* The scribes who copied the texts on the scrolls each had a unique handwriting style, just as people do today. Paleographers study the bookhand (shape and size of written characters) and are able to identify different scribes' styles and, to a great extent, determine which fragments belong together.

3. *Horizontal lines.* Scribes or copyists prepared the leather scrolls for inscription by creating horizontal lines on the leather, similar in some respects to the lined paper of modern times. The horizontal lines served to guide the hand of the scribe as he copied down the characters. The space between lines often varied, a characteristic that has helped scholars determine which fragments belong together.

4. *Scribal markings.* Many scribes placed various unique markings in the margins of the leather or between the lines of the text. Such scribal markings provide additional clues to how the fragments should be pieced together.

5. *Textual clues.* The words on a fragment may facilitate its identification and positioning among related fragments, especially if the words belong to a previously known text. For instance, a fragment with the words "every tree of the garden"

A scholar examines scroll fragments. Photograph courtesy of the estate of John M. Allegro.

(from Genesis 2:16) alert the scholar to place the fragment with other fragments belonging to the Old Testament book of Genesis.

6. *Material join.* A "material join" is (1) when two fragments have complementing edges (like two adjoining pieces of a jigsaw puzzle) or (2) when one fragment has half of a single word (such as *Melchi-*) and a second fragment has the other half of the same word (such as *-zedek*). Scholars are able to join the two fragments together to read *Melchizedek.*

The sorting process is often a painstaking and tedious task. As Professor Frank Moore Cross explains, "A single fragment may require many hours of study before it receives exact identification and is placed in a slowly growing column of a manuscript."[30] However, the results of joining one fragment with another provide great satisfaction to the scholar.

25. Who is translating the scrolls?

The Dead Sea Scrolls translation team began as a small group of scholars in the early 1950s but expanded to approximately sixty members by the mid-1990s.

Under the direction of Roland de Vaux, a Dominican priest and biblical scholar who was director of the École Biblique in Jerusalem in the 1950s, assignments were made to prepare, sort, and publish the scrolls and fragments. Those asked to do so included de Vaux's Catholic associates at the École Biblique: Pierre Benoit, Josef T. Milik, and Maurice Baillet. Later, because of the enormity of the task, a small team was formed from Christian institutions, so that four Catholics and four Protestants became the official team of editors.[31] Over the decades the team expanded, especially under the leadership of Editor in Chief John Strugnell in the late 1980s, followed by Editor in Chief Emanuel Tov in the 1990s. Under the direction of Tov, the official team expanded to some sixty translators, where it remains at the time of this writing.

26. Are members of the LDS Church translating the scrolls?

Until the early 1990s, the role of Latter-day Saint scholars in Dead Sea Scrolls research was modest, although Brigham Young University professor Hugh W. Nibley produced valuable studies on the scrolls. Since 1994, however, BYU scholars have been much more active in scrolls research.

In January 1994 Professor Emanuel Tov, editor in chief of the Dead Sea Scrolls project, invited Donald W. Parry of BYU's Department of Asian and Near Eastern Languages to become a member of the international team of editors working on the scrolls. Parry was assigned to work with Professor Frank Moore Cross on the biblical books of Samuel. Later that same year, Tov invited BYU professors Dana M. Pike, David Rolph

Seely, and Andrew C. Skinner (all from the Department of Ancient Scripture) to join the international team. Pike and Skinner were assigned to work on miscellaneous fragments, and Seely was invited to work with Professor Moshe Weinfeld on selected hymns. The translations of Parry, Pike, Seely, and Skinner will be published in the official publication of the Dead Sea Scrolls, a series titled Discoveries in the Judaean Desert, published by Oxford University Press.

Professors Donald W. Parry (left) and Stephen D. Ricks engaged in research on the scrolls.

27. How are the translations controlled or reviewed for accuracy?

The scholarly community has rigid controls in place to ensure the quality of work conducted on the Dead Sea Scrolls.

These controls include careful review, editing, and proofreading of manuscripts before they are published in the authoritative Discoveries in the Judaean Desert series. Editors in chief of the series oversee the work of the scholars and translators so that high standards of excellence remain at all stages of production.

28. Where can I find accurate English translations of the scrolls?

Recently two fine English translations of the nonbiblical scrolls have been published: Geza Vermes, *The Complete Dead Sea Scrolls in English* (New York: Penguin, 1997), and Florentino García Martínez, *The Dead Sea Scrolls Translated: The Qumran Texts in English* (2nd ed., Leiden: E. J. Brill, 1994). Designed and priced for the lay reader, both volumes are priced under $30.

The official transcriptions and translations of the scrolls appear in the official series Discoveries in the Judaean Desert, published by Oxford University Press. The individual books in the series, however, are designed and formatted for scholars and advanced researchers and are quite expensive, sometimes selling for as much as $150 per volume.

29. When will the scrolls be translated and made available to the public?

All of the nonbiblical texts of the scrolls have been translated into English and are available to the lay reader in single-volume works, such as those identified in question 28. Most of the scholarly editions of those same texts appear in the series Discoveries in the Judaean Desert, often abbreviated to DJD (see question 28). The scholarly editions of the remaining texts will be published in the DJD series in the next two or three years. Many of the biblical texts have been or will be published in that series as well.

30. Why has it taken so long to release and publish the scrolls?

Since the last of the Dead Sea Scrolls was discovered in 1956, the question is often asked, Why has it taken so long to publish the scrolls? Many people have responded to this question. A summary of their reasons follows.

1. Lack of scholarly access to the scrolls. Geza Vermes, an eminent scrolls scholar, cites "scholarly mismanagement and irresponsibility" as the reason behind a half century of delays in publishing the scrolls. He faults Father Roland de Vaux, the one-time leader of the translation team, for imposing "rules of secrecy on the project that limited access to the manuscripts to the members of the international team, and prevented other scholars from working on them."[32] Most scholars generally were not permitted access to the scrolls until the early 1990s, at which time the pace of the translation and publication of the scrolls increased at an accelerated rate.

2. Limited access to the scrolls. A number of the scholars assigned to translate the scrolls were distracted by university assignments and other scholarly projects that limited the time they could work on the scrolls. Moreover, limited access to the documents meant that professors could work only in the summer, when their teaching assignments allowed them to spend time in the Middle East.

3. Enormity of the task. The great number of manuscripts and fragments, combined with their poor condition, created a task of gigantic dimensions, which included the identification and piecing together of thousands of small scroll fragments. The original members of the translation team underestimated the amount of work required to translate the scrolls, a matter of too much being expected of too few.

4. Inadequate funding. Dead Sea Scrolls translators and scholars often lack adequate financial support to carry on their work. They usually are required to finance their own work and travel to Jerusalem, often with an extended stay in that city. Such economic challenges create hardships and delay the publication of the scrolls.

5. Scroll conspiracies. Some publications have claimed that the Vatican, the Great Rabbinate, the Council of Churches, other religious institutions, or certain authorities have suppressed the publication of the scrolls because of the fear that the scrolls had the potential to undermine the faith of Christians or Jews. Such claims are untrue, founded on sensationalism or misinformation. Florentino García Martínez describes two versions of this inaccuracy that have prevailed in the last few years:

> The content of this myth in its crudest form can be expressed as follows. Among the Dead Sea Scrolls there are many texts the publication of which would pose a great danger for the established religions, Judaism as well as Christianity. These alleged texts would allow the falsehood of both Christianity and Judaism as a religion to be demonstrated. For this reason, the religious authorities (Jewish and Christian alike) have prevented their publication until now. In another version of the myth, the religious authorities (the Great Rabbinate, the Vatican or the Council of Churches) are not involved. Instead, the actual research scholars responsible for publication (some of whom are priests or ministers) willingly censored certain texts which offended their religious sensibilities or delayed their publication to prevent the harm they could do to the faithful.[33]

The real explanations for the delay in the publication of the texts are many and varied. Our strong inclination is to accept all of the reasons except the last one, the sensationalist rumors concerning the content of the scrolls.

PART IV

THE DEAD SEA SCROLLS
AND MODERN TECHNOLOGY

31. What is the FARMS Dead Sea Scrolls computer database?

The Foundation for Ancient Research and Mormon Studies (FARMS) at Brigham Young University, in collaboration with other institutions, has developed a computerized library of the Dead Sea Scrolls called the *Dead Sea Scrolls Electronic Reference Library.* It includes eight hundred photographs of nearly all of the nonbiblical scrolls, the texts of those scrolls written in Hebrew characters, an English translation, a catalog of the Dead Sea Scrolls, and related materials such as the Hebrew Bible and the Septuagint (the Greek translation of the Old Testament). This state-of-the-art research tool on CD-ROM enables scholars, researchers, students, and other interested persons to gain access to and study the scrolls on their personal computers. Among other features, the sophisticated software links the scroll fragments and images with their corresponding texts, and the user can display, enlarge, and scroll this material in separate windows, as well as conduct word or phrase searches.

32. What about DNA research and the scrolls?

Scott R. Woodward, a geneticist in the Department of Microbiology at Brigham Young University, is assisting the international team of translators by using DNA analysis to determine which parchment scroll fragments came from the same animal and therefore belong together.

Woodward, with the cooperation of Gila Kahila, Patricia Smith, Charles Greenblatt, Joe Zias, and Magen Broshi, began DNA testing on the scrolls and fragments there during the summer of 1994. He explains how DNA analysis works:

> Because [the Dead Sea Scrolls] parchments were produced from animal skins it is possible that they would contain remnant DNA molecules. Within the last decade new techniques in molecular biology have been developed that have made it possible to recover DNA from ancient sources. The molecular analysis of ancient DNA (aDNA) from the Judean desert parchment fragments would enable us to establish a genetic signature unique for each manuscript. The precision of the DNA analysis will allow us to identify at least three levels of hierarchy: the species, population, and individual animal from which the parchment was produced.[34]

DNA analysis has already identified the animal species from which the leather used to create the scrolls was produced: at least two parchments were created from either an ibex or gazelle; other parchments came from wild or domestic goats. DNA analysis will also assist scholars in determining whether the library of scrolls came from the immediate region of Qumran and the Dead Sea or from other areas of ancient Palestine.

PART V

THE DEAD SEA SCROLLS
AND THE OLD TESTAMENT

33. Which Old Testament books were discovered among the scrolls?

Approximately two hundred of the Dead Sea Scrolls represent books from the Old Testament, such as Genesis, Exodus, Samuel, Isaiah, and Jeremiah. Most of these scrolls were damaged over time and now exist as fragments. In some cases, multiple copies of portions of a single work have been found, including fifteen copies of Genesis, eight copies of Numbers, two copies of Joshua, three copies of Judges, twenty-one copies of Isaiah, six copies of Jeremiah, six copies of Ezekiel, thirty-six copies of Psalms, two copies of Proverbs, and four copies of Ruth.[35] All of the books of the Old Testament, except the book of Esther, were discovered among the Dead Sea Scrolls. Some scholars, noting that Purim (the festival celebrating the deliverance of the Jews exiled in Persia) is conspicuously absent from Qumran's calendrical texts, have suggested that the book of Esther may have been deliberately excluded from the Qumran community because (1) its theme of retaliation is contrary to teachings in the scrolls, (2) it makes no reference to God, and (3) Esther, a Jew, married a Persian king, a union that may have been repugnant to the conservative group at Qumran.[36]

34. What is the *Great Isaiah Scroll?*

The *Great Isaiah Scroll* was one of the initial seven Dead Sea Scrolls discovered, and because of its beauty and completeness, it is perhaps the most famous of the biblical scrolls. It was found wrapped in a linen cloth and concealed in a large clay jar in Cave 1. Containing all sixty-six chapters of the book of Isaiah, the scroll consists of seventeen pieces of sheepskin sewn together to form a scroll measuring 24.5 feet in length and 10.5 inches in height. The scroll was prepared in approximately 150 B.C.

The scribe who copied the book of Isaiah onto the scroll was quite careless in his work, erring in numerous places. The first error is located in the first line of text, where the scribe misspelled Isaiah's name. He corrected his own errors on a

Recovered from Cave 1 in 1947, the *Great Isaiah Scroll* contains the complete text of the book of Isaiah. Photograph by John C. Trever.

number of occasions by writing the corrections between the lines or in the margins. The scroll contains numerous scribal markings that may mark passages that were important to the Qumran community. The scroll shows much evidence of use, as it was well-worn before it was stored in the jar.

A column from the *Great Isaiah Scroll* showing scribal markings, such as the two x's at the left of the column.

This scroll is extremely important to the study of the Bible because it is approximately one thousand years older than other Hebrew copies of Isaiah. Although most of the readings of the scroll are the same as those of the traditional Hebrew Bible (the Masoretic Text), there are a number of important variant readings that have been included in modern translations of Isaiah. For example, Isaiah 33:8, as translated in the King James Version of the Bible, reads:

The highways lie waste, the wayfaring man ceaseth: he hath broken the covenant, he hath despised the cities, he regardeth no man.

The Isaiah scroll reads:

The highways lie waste, the wayfaring man ceaseth: he hath broken the covenant, he hath despised the witnesses, he regardeth no man.

The Isaiah scroll reads *witnesses* rather than *cities*, thus presenting a more accurate, superior reading.

35. Does the text of the *Great Isaiah Scroll* support the Isaiah passages in the Book of Mormon that differ from those in the King James Bible?

The Book of Mormon contains lengthy quotations from Isaiah (see, for example, 2 Nephi 12–24). In many instances the wording of corresponding Isaiah passages in the King James Version of the Bible (KJV) and in the Book of Mormon differs. To date, no one has completed a comprehensive study comparing the Isaiah scroll from Cave 1 with the Isaiah passages in the Book of Mormon Isaiah. In 1981, however, John Tvedtnes[37] conducted a serviceable preliminary study by comparing the Isaiah passages in the Book of Mormon with those in the KJV, the Hebrew Bible, the scrolls found at Qumran (notably the *Great Isaiah Scroll,* which contains all sixty-six chapters of Isaiah), and other ancient versions of Isaiah.

Several readings of Isaiah in the Book of Mormon are supported by the Isaiah scroll. The following representative examples of these parallels have been adapted from Tvedtnes's work.

1. In many cases passages in the Isaiah scroll and in the Book of Mormon contain the conjunction *and,* which is lacking in the corresponding KJV text. Compare the following:

"and they declare their sin as Sodom, they hide it not" (KJV, Isaiah 3:9)

"and they declare their sin as Sodom, *and* they hide it not" (Isaiah scroll, Isaiah 3:9)

"and doth declare their sin to be even as Sodom, *and* they cannot hide it" (Book of Mormon, 2 Nephi 13:9=Isaiah 3:9)

2. Second Nephi 24:32 lacks the word *one,* which appears in Isaiah 14:32. The Book of Mormon version thus makes *messengers* the subject of the verb *answer.* The Hebrew Bible uses a singular verb, but the Isaiah scroll uses the plural, in agreement with the Book of Mormon:

"What shall *one* then answer the messengers of the nation?" (KJV, Isaiah 14:32)

"What shall then answer the messengers of the nations?" (Isaiah scroll, Isaiah 14:32)

"What shall then answer the messengers of the nations?" (Book of Mormon, 2 Nephi 24:32=Isaiah 14:32)

3. In the KJV, Isaiah 48:11 reads, "for how should my name be polluted?" while 1 Nephi 20:11 reads, "for I will not suffer my name to be polluted." The Isaiah scroll supports the Book of Mormon by having the verb in the first person, as follows:

"for how should my name be polluted?" (KJV, Isaiah 48:11)

"for *I will not suffer* my name to be polluted" (Isaiah scroll, Isaiah 14:32)

"for *I will not suffer* my name to be polluted" (Book of Mormon, 1 Nephi 20:11=Isaiah 48:11)

4. In the KJV, Isaiah 50:2 reads, "their fish stinketh, because there is no water," and the Isaiah scroll reads, "their fish dry up because there is no water." Second Nephi 7:2 essentially preserves the verb *stinketh* from the KJV and the phrasal verb *dry*

up from the Isaiah scroll: "their fish to stink because the waters are dried up."

5. Often a singular noun in the KJV is represented by a plural noun in the Book of Mormon. One example of this appears in Isaiah 9:9, where the KJV reads "inhabitant" and 2 Nephi 19:9 reads "inhabitants." The Isaiah scroll supports the reading of the Book of Mormon with its reading of "inhabitants":

"and the inhabitant of Samaria" (KJV, Isaiah 9:9)

"and the *inhabitants* of Samaria" (Isaiah scroll, Isaiah 9:9)

"and the *inhabitants* of Samaria" (Book of Mormon, 2 Nephi 19:9=Isaiah 9:9)

These examples of variant readings in which the Isaiah passages in the Book of Mormon agree with the Isaiah scroll but not with the KJV could be multiplied.

36. Did the people of Qumran have books in their scriptures not found in our present Old Testament?

It is not known exactly which books the people of Qumran considered to be scripture, although it is almost certain that they accepted all the books of the Old Testament to be such. It is quite possible that they accepted other books into their canon of scripture, such as the *Temple Scroll* and the book of *Jubilees*.[38]

37. How have the biblical scrolls and fragments influenced the English translation of the Bible?

Many contemporary translation committees of the Bible pay special attention to the Dead Sea Scrolls biblical texts and incorporate many new readings into their translations. A look at the book of 1 Samuel will show the importance that translation committees place on the scrolls. The 1986 edition of the

New International Version (NIV) accepts 15 readings from the Dead Sea Scrolls texts of 1 Samuel that do not agree with the Hebrew Bible. For example, the NIV prefers the reading "with a three-year-old bull," found in the Dead Sea Scrolls, over the traditional reading of the Hebrew Bible, "with three bulls" (compare 1 Samuel 1:24 KJV). The translation committee of the *New American Bible* (1970) was even more accommodating, preferring 230 Dead Sea Scrolls readings from 1 Samuel over the Hebrew Bible. The following list[39] features six prominent English translations of the book of 1 Samuel. The number next to them indicates how many times respective translation committees chose the Dead Sea Scrolls biblical text of 1 Samuel over the traditional Hebrew Bible.

New International Version	15
Today's English Version	51
Revised Standard Version	about 60
New Revised Standard Version	about 110
New English Bible	160
New American Bible	230

Yet many other translation committees, in preparing their new translations or revisions of previous translations, have disregarded the variant readings of the Dead Sea Scrolls. For instance, the *New King James Version* of 1982 prefers one variant reading from the Dead Sea Scrolls book of 1 Samuel; in fact, it relies on the Dead Sea Scrolls on only six occasions in the entire Old Testament (in Deuteronomy 32:43; 1 Samuel 1:24; Isaiah 10:16; 22:8; 38:14; 49:5).[40]

Generally, though, recent translation committees have examined and subsequently integrated many variant readings of the Dead Sea Scrolls into their translations. According to Harold Scanlin, a translation adviser for the United Bible Societies, "Every major Bible translation published since 1950 has claimed to have taken into account the textual evidence of the Dead Sea Scrolls."[41]

Many of these English translations have gone through subsequent revisions to incorporate the variant readings gained from recent scholarship. For instance, the *Revised Standard Version* (1952) is now the *New Revised Standard Version* (1990), the *New English Bible* (1970) has become the *Revised English Bible* (1989), the *Jerusalem Bible* (1966) is now the *New Jerusalem Bible* (1985), and the *New American Bible* (1970) is going through a major revision at the present time. It is anticipated that the translation committees will accept more variant readings from the biblical scrolls and fragments in the coming years.

38. Are there passages missing from our Bible that were discovered among the scrolls?

Scribal error has caused words and entire phrases to be omitted from, changed, or added to the books of the Old Testament. For instance, James C. VanderKam notes that one Hebrew version of the five books of Moses (Genesis, Exodus, Leviticus, Numbers, and Deuteronomy) differs from another Hebrew version in "some six thousand readings; most of these are minor matters such as different spellings of words."[42]

Copies of a few of the books of the Old Testament, such as 1 and 2 Samuel discovered in Cave 4, have scores of words and phrases that apparently have been lost or changed through scribal error.[43] A striking example of an entire verse of scripture that was lost more than two thousand years ago has been discovered in the Dead Sea Scrolls texts of Samuel.[44] The new verse presents some forty-nine Hebrew words that were missing in the Hebrew Bible. The missing verse reads as follows:

> And Nahash, king of the children of Ammon, oppressed harshly the Gadites and the Reubenites. He would gouge out

the right eye of each of them and would not grant Israel a deliverer. No one was left of the Israelites across the Jordan whose right eye Nahash, King of the Ammonites, had not gouged out. But there were seven thousand men who had fled from the Ammonites and had entered Jabesh-gilead.[45]

With this verse in place at 1 Samuel 11:1, a better transition occurs from the final verse in chapter 10 to the first verse in chapter 11, and the context for the story of King Nahash falls into place. The verse also assists students of the Bible in understanding the situation described in chapter 11 concerning the advance of Nahash and his troops against Jabesh-gilead and the Israelites. It was the plan of Nahash to make a treaty with the Israelites who were dwelling in Jabesh-gilead, under the condition that he be allowed to "gouge out the right eye of each person in the city," rendering them helpless in rebelling against him. The story turns out well for the Israelites, however, for they rally around King Saul and the prophet Samuel (see 1 Samuel 11:5–7), and together they slay a number of Ammonites and cause the remainder to flee. Samuel and Saul give credit to the Lord for their victory.

There are many other passages that have been discovered

A scroll fragment from the book of Samuel reveals the missing text shown here that improves the transition between 1 Samuel 10 and 11. Photography courtesy of Ancient Biblical Manuscript Center, with permission from the Israel Antiquities Authority.

among the Dead Sea Scrolls biblical texts that perhaps are biblical in nature, such as the psalms called the *Prayer for Deliverance* and *Hymn to the Creator*. Newly discovered prose texts were also found, including *An Account of David's Poems, The Prayer of Nabonidus,* and *A Jeremiah Apocryphon.* One newly discovered text is the *Apostrophe to Zion,* a beautiful psalm that sets forth the wonders of Zion. The first half of this psalm reads:

> I will remember you, O Zion, for a blessing;
> with all my might I love you;
> your memory is to be blessed for ever.
> Your hope is great, O Zion;
> Peace and your awaited salvation will come.
> Generation after generation shall dwell in you,
> and generations of the pious shall be your ornament.
> They who desire the day of your salvation
> shall rejoice in the greatness of your glory.
> They shall be suckled on the fullness of your glory,
> and in your beautiful streets they shall make tinkling sounds.
> You shall remember the pious deeds of your prophets,
> and shall glorify yourselves in the deeds of your pious ones.
> Cleanse violence from your midst;
> lying and iniquity, may they be cut off from you.
> Your sons shall rejoice within you,
> and your cherished ones shall be joined to you.
> How much they have hoped in your salvation,
> and how much your perfect ones have mourned for you?
> Your hope, O Zion, shall not perish,
> and your expectation will not be forgotten.
> (*Apostrophe to Zion* 12:1–9)

PART VI

THE DEAD SEA SCROLLS
AND THE NEW TESTAMENT

39. Were books of the New Testament discovered among the scrolls?

Not a single copy of a New Testament book was found among the Dead Sea Scrolls. The reason for this is twofold: first, the group that inhabited Qumran was *not* Christian; second, many or most of the texts belonging to the corpus of the Dead Sea Scrolls were created and copied before the rise of Christianity in the first century A.D.

40. Are there any references to Christ or Christianity in the scrolls?

Most of the Qumran writings were written between the third and first centuries B.C., long before the advent of Christianity, and thus contain no historical references to Christ or Christianity. An early scholar of the Dead Sea Scrolls, G. Lankester Harding, once suggested that Jesus Christ studied with the people of Qumran, but this suggestion is sensationalistic and without basis in fact. Jesus Christ is not identified, explicitly or implicitly, in the nonbiblical scrolls. Nevertheless, the scrolls do provide much information about Judaism and the religious scene of the period, from which Christianity was established.

This scroll fragment, known as 4Q175 *Testimonia,* assembles quotations from the Old Testament (Hebrew Bible) that pertain to the Messiah. Photograph courtesy of David W. Hawkinson.

41. Did the Qumran community accept Jesus Christ when he came?

As a group, the Essenes of Qumran did not accept Jesus as the Messiah during his mortal ministry. Brigham Young University professor David Rolph Seely has pointed out that in A.D. 68 the Essenes "were still at Qumran awaiting divine intervention on their behalf when their community was destroyed by the Romans."[46] It is possible that a few members of the Qumran community hearkened to the voice of John the Baptist or Jesus Christ and joined the Christian flock, but there is no evidence to support this idea.

42. Is John the Baptist identified in the scrolls?

No references to John the Baptist exist in the scrolls. Some scholars,[47] however, believe that John may have been affiliated with Qumran as he preached near the Jordan River, but there is not sufficient evidence of this. Also, a few scholars have compared John's baptisms "in the wilderness" to the immersion rites of those at Qumran, but John's baptisms were for "the remission of sins" (Mark 1:4) while the ritual of those at Qumran was for other purposes, as set forth in the *Community Rule:* "They shall not enter the water to partake of the pure Meal of the men of holiness, for they shall not be cleansed unless they turn from their wickedness" (*Community Rule* 5:13–14; compare 4:20–21). Most significantly, John testified of Jesus Christ, whom the Qumranites did not accept as their Messiah.

43. Are there similarities between the beliefs of Christianity and those of the Qumran group?

Because members of the Qumran community were Jews living before the advent of Christianity, little can be learned from the scrolls about Christianity. However, a few approximate parallels and correspondences between early Christianity and the beliefs of the Qumran community may be drawn from the Dead Sea Scrolls, including:

1. Immersion in water. The scrolls mention water rites required of those who enter the community for the first time or reenter it after a period of separation. Like the baptism of the early Christians, this rite was performed by immersion, but unlike baptism, the water rites had nothing to do with Jesus Christ or the remission of sins.

2. *Healing through the laying on of hands.* The New Testament refers to the healing of the sick by the laying on of hands (see Mark 6:5; Luke 4:40; 13:11–13), a practice that corresponds to a passage in the *Genesis Apocryphon.* According to this text, Pharaoh, king of Egypt, was suffering from "scourges and afflictions." He called upon his "magicians" and "healers" to heal him, but they failed to do so; he then called upon Abraham, who healed the pharaoh by the laying on of hands. Abraham explains, "So I prayed [for him] . . . and I laid my hands on his [head]; and the scourge departed from him and the evil [spirit] was expelled [from him], and he lived" (*Genesis Apocryphon* 20:21–22, 28–29).

3. *Twelve and three.* According to the *Community Rule,* the Qumran community had at its head a group of twelve men, who themselves were directed by three:

> In the Council of the Community there shall be twelve men and three Priests, perfectly versed in all that is revealed of the Law, whose works shall be truth, righteousness, justice, loving-kindness and humility. They shall preserve the faith in the Land with steadfastness and meekness and shall atone for sin by the practice of justice and by suffering the sorrows of affliction. They shall walk with all men according to the standard of truth and the rule of the time.
>
> When these are in Israel, the Council of the Community shall be established in truth. . . . They shall be witnesses to the truth at the Judgement, and shall be the elect of Goodwill who shall atone for the Land and pay to the wicked their reward. (*Community Rule* 8:1–7)

The number twelve corresponds with the number of the apostles whom Jesus selected; but the twelve men who directed the Council of the Community were not apostles, nor did they possess the powers to cast out unclean spirits, heal the sick, and perform other such acts (see Matthew 10:1–5).

4. Beatitudes. The beatitudes of the Sermon on the Mount (see Matthew 5:3–11), each of which begin with the word *Blessed,* correspond in some ways to the beatitudes discovered in the scrolls. A Cave 4 fragment called *Beatitudes* reads in part:

> Blessed are those who hold to her (Wisdom's) precepts
> and do not hold to the ways of iniquity.
> Blessed are those who rejoice in her,
> and do not burst forth in ways of folly.
> Blessed are those who seek her with pure hands,
> and do not pursue her with a treacherous heart.
> Blessed is the man who has attained Wisdom,
> and walks in the Law of the Most High.
> (*Beatitudes* 2:1–3)

5. Light and Darkness. The apostle John's writings contain many teachings regarding light and darkness. As recorded in John 12:35–36: "Then Jesus said unto them, Yet a little while is the light with you. Walk while ye have the light, lest darkness come upon you: for he that walketh in darkness knoweth not whither he goeth. While ye have light, believe in the light, that ye may be the children of light" (see John 1:4–5; 3:19; 8:12; 1 John 1:5–6).

Professor Julio Trebolle Barrera of the Universidad Complutense of Madrid sees definite parallels between these teachings and those in the scrolls that speak of "spirits of light and darkness," "source of light," "source of darkness," "Prince of Lights," "paths of light," "Angel of Darkness," "paths of darkness," and "sons of light" (*Community Rule* 3:19–26).[48]

6. Other similarities. Julio Trebolle Barrera discusses several additional parallels between the Qumran texts and the beliefs of Christianity, including the two groups' approach to

wealth, their beliefs regarding divorce, the communal meal and
Last Supper, the bid for perfection, disciplinary action against
those who break rules, the idea of the Creator, overlapping
concepts from Paul's epistles and the Qumran texts, and the
way that the expression "Son of God" is used.[49]

Notwithstanding the correspondences between the two
groups, there are many points of contrast that are noted in the
following question.

44. Are there differences between the beliefs of Christianity and those of the Qumran group?

Parallels and correspondences between groups can be mis-
leading if the differences are not also pointed out. The foremost difference between the Qumran community and Christians
is the Christian belief in Jesus Christ and his life, ministry, divine nature, and atoning sacrifice. The Qumran community
did *not* share the following Christian beliefs: Jesus is "the me-
diator of life" (Galatians 3:19–20 Joseph Smith Translation),
the "Lord of lords" (Revelation 17:14), "the true and living
God" (1 Nephi 17:30), the "lawgiver" (Doctrine and Covenants
38:22; compare 3 Nephi 15:9), "the Lord God Almighty; the
Lord Jehovah" (Exodus 6:3 JST), the "Holy One of Israel"
(2 Nephi 9:41), and the "Redeemer of Israel" (1 Nephi 21:7).

Although the community at Qumran held a belief in a
messianic figure (or more than one such figure), Jesus Christ
was not their Messiah. The Book of Mormon is explicit in
naming Christ as the Messiah: "For according to the words of
the prophets, the Messiah cometh in six hundred years from
the time that my father left Jerusalem; and according to the
words of the prophets, and also the word of the angel of God,
his name shall be Jesus Christ, the Son of God" (2 Nephi 25:19).

Furthermore, the Qumran community did not share with

the Christians beliefs in the plan of salvation, aspects of church organization, priesthood offices, the Second Coming, a living prophet, the bestowal of the gift of the Holy Ghost through the laying on of hands, the gift of tongues and interpretation of tongues, other gifts of revelation and of the Spirit, and numerous other doctrines that were part of the early Christian church and that are now part of the Church of Jesus of Christ of Latter-day Saints.

PART VII

Specific Texts of the
Dead Sea Scrolls

45. What is the *Commentary on Habakkuk?*

The *Commentary on Habakkuk,* found in Cave 1, is a verse-by-verse commentary covering the first two chapters of the book of Habakkuk. This commentary, also known as the *Pesher Habakkuk,* dates to the Herodian period (30–1 B.C.), although the composition itself dates to an earlier period. According to the commentary, the mysteries of the Lord's prophets were revealed to Qumran's Teacher of Righteousness and Habakkuk's prophecy was interpreted in relation to the people of Qumran in the last days. For example, we read in the *Pesher Habakkuk:*

> And God told Habakkuk to write what was going to happen
> to the last generation, but he did not let him know the end
> of the age. And as for what he says: [Hab 2:2] So that the one
> who reads it /may run/. Its interpretation concerns the
> Teacher of Righteousness, to whom God has disclosed all
> the mysteries of the words of his servants, the prophets.
> [Hab 2:3]⁵⁰

46. What is the *Genesis Apocryphon?*

The *Genesis Apocryphon* retells and amplifies many of the events recorded in Genesis. The first readable passage of this damaged scroll describes Lamech's response to the news that his wife, Bitenosh (who is not named in the Bible), is with child. The passage then continues with the story of Noah. The best-preserved sections enlarge upon the story of Abram and Sarai (Abraham and Sarah) in Egypt and of Abram's calling Sarai his sister, found in Genesis 12:10–20.

47. What is the *Messianic Apocalypse?*

Interest has recently been directed to the so-called *Messianic Apocalypse,* parts of which may be translated as follows:

... [the hea]vens and earth will listen to His Messiah, and none therein will stray from the commandments of the holy ones.

Seekers of the Lord, strengthen yourself in His service!

All you hopeful in (your) heart, will you not find the Lord in this?

For the Lord will consider the pious *(hasidim)* and call the righteous by name.

Over the poor His spirit will hover and will renew the faithful with His power.

And He will glorify the pious on the throne of the eternal Kingdom.

He who liberates the captives, restores sight to the blind, straightens the b[ent] (Ps. cxlvi, 7–8).

And f[or] ever I will clea[ve to the h]opeful and in His mercy...

And the fr[uit...] will not be delayed for anyone

And the Lord will accomplish glorious things which have never been as [He...]

For He will heal the wounded, and revive the dead and bring good news to the poor (Isa. lxi., 1).

. . . He will lead the uprooted and knowledge . . . and smoke (?) . . .

This fragment is particularly interesting because it may shed further light on the Qumran community's view of their messiah, a subject that continues to be intensely debated. Some scholars interpret the writings from the Dead Sea as indicating a single messianic figure, while other scholars find evidence for a belief in two messiahs, one priestly and one royal. While the majority of messianic references in the Dead Sea Scrolls are clearly singular in form, there is one example where the word *messiah* is plural and appears to refer to two separate messianic figures.

48. What is the *Damascus Document?*

This text has been identified by several names over the years, including the *Damascus Covenant,* the *Damascus Rule,* and the *Zadokite Fragments.* It is unique because a copy was first found in an old synagogue in Cairo, Egypt, in 1896, long before the Dead Sea Scrolls were discovered. The manuscripts are known as the *Damascus Document* because Damascus is prominently mentioned as the place where the group originated. While Damascus could refer to the actual city in Syria, most scholars believe it is a code or symbolic name for a "city" in the wilderness, possibly Qumran. Ten copies of the *Damascus Document* have been found in the Qumran caves.

A copy of the *Damascus Document* from Cave 4 shows that the community at Qumran had a version somewhat longer than the manuscripts found in Cairo. The document consists of two parts: an exhortation and a legal section (or body of laws). In the exhortation, the new members of the covenant are encouraged, through the examples of reward and punishment in Israel's history, to be obedient to the ways of God and the guidelines of the covenant. This section of the document has been very important in deciphering some of the early history of the Qumran community. In the legal section, certain laws are laid out, such as laws for the Sabbath and for ritual purity. This section is divided into five parts: entry into the covenant, code of conduct, ritual, organization, and penal code.

Some differences in the rules and regulations of the *Damascus Document* and those of the *Community Rule* initially led scholars to believe that the *Damascus Document* pertained to a completely different movement than that found at Qumran. However, references in the document to "camps," "the assembly of the towns of Israel," and "the assembly of the camps" suggest that the rules contained therein are for regulating different segments of the movement, which was spread throughout the land. Thus, in the *Damascus Document,* members of the covenant community outside of Qumran are understood to be living among people who are not members of that community; and marriage, which is not even mentioned in the *Community Rule* (members of the Qumran group are thought to have been celibate), is an assumed part of life within the covenant community.

Yet while the *Damascus Document* provides regulations for adherents living outside of Qumran, it seems to acknowledge Qumran as the center of the community. For example, the Teacher of Righteousness is looked upon as the leader of the group, and the community is repeatedly referred to as being from the land of Damascus (a possible code name for Qumran, as explained earlier). Also, the rules found in the *Damascus Document* do not seem to be as strict as those in the

Community Rule, leading to the belief that the group at Qumran followed a stricter order of living within the group.[51]

49. What is the *Community Rule,* or *Manual of Discipline?*

The central organizational document found among the Dead Sea Scrolls, and one unique to the Qumran community, is the *Community Rule* (or *Manual of Discipline,* as it is still popularly known). It was designed for a faithful "remnant" of Israel engaged in preparing the "way in the desert" for the kingdom of God and for God's triumph over the forces of evil. The document contains a preamble explaining the purpose of the group and sets forth its basic constitution, including the requirements for entrance into the community, the procedures for admission, the various classes or ranks within the community, the regulations governing the relations of community members, the conduct of communal meals, and items concerning military service, education, and eligibility for office.

The *Community Rule* also provides a list of penalties (ranging from loss of rations to expulsion from the community) for various types of infractions, suggesting something of the strictness of the group. For example, the list of penalties instructs that

> Whoever has deliberately lied shall do penance for six months.
> Whoever has deliberately insulted his companion unjustly shall do penance for one year and shall be excluded.
> Whoever has deliberately deceived his companion by word or by deed shall do penance for six months. . . .
> Whoever has borne malice against his companion unjustly shall do penance for six months/one year; and likewise, whoever has taken revenge in any matter whatever.
> Whoever has spoken foolishly: three months.

Whoever has interrupted his companion whilst speaking: ten days.

Whoever has lain down to sleep during an Assembly of the Congregation: thirty days. And likewise, whoever has left, without reason, an Assembly of the Congregation as many as three times during one Assembly, shall do penance for ten days. But if he has departed whilst they were standing he shall do penance for thirty days.

(*Community Rule* 7:4–14)

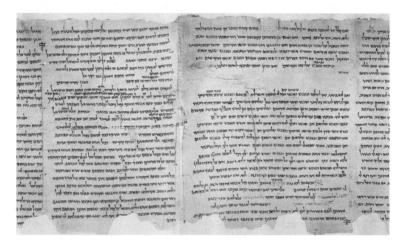

An excerpt from a replica of the *Community Rule* scroll, which sets forth the bylaws of the Qumran community.

In many respects the *Community Rule* displays parallels to community regulations for later Christian groups, whose documents include the *Didache,* the *Apostolic Constitutions,* the *Didascalia,* and the *Rule of Benedict.* All products of the early Christian centuries, these documents, like the *Community Rule,* reflect a concern with providing a constitution for the communities as well as a pattern for daily living.

50. Is the *Community Rule* a kind of initiation text?

The *Community Rule* contains the following basic steps of initiation into the Qumran community: an expression of willingness to enter the covenant, a collective confession of wrongdoing and an acknowledgment of God's mercy, and the blessing of those who enter into the covenant.

Moshe Weinfeld identifies six characteristics of this entrance process that are similar to the practices of other societies in the Hellenistic world: oath of admission, registration, examination, decision by lot, probationary period, and submission of personal property. He points out many similarities between the Qumran community and "guilds and religious associations of the Hellenistic-Roman Period."[52]

51. What is the *Rule of the Congregation?*

Appended to the *Community Rule* scroll is the *Rule of the Congregation* (or *Messianic Rule*). Whereas the *Community Rule* seems more devoted to the real-life organization and management of the affairs of the community, the *Rule of the Congregation* served a different purpose. According to Geza Vermes, "(1) it was intended for 'all the congregation in the last days'; (2) it is a Rule for a Community adapted to the requirements of the messianic war against the nations; (3) it refers to the presence of the Priest and the Messiah of Israel at the Council, and at the Meal."[53]

52. What is the *Copper Scroll?*

Among the most puzzling of the Dead Sea Scrolls is the *Copper Scroll,* first published by Josef T. Milik in 1962 in the third volume of the Discoveries in the Judaean Desert series.[54]

The *Copper Scroll* is extraordinary for several reasons: its unique orthography (method of spelling), its use of a Hebrew script and dialect that are unlike that of any other scrolls, its use of metal as a means of textual transmission, and its contents regarding deposits of treasures. It is not known who created or owned this scroll.

The *Copper Scroll* apparently was formed from a single plaque of copper-based metal. Inscribed thereon is a list of sixty-four deposits of gold, silver, aromatic spices, and manu-

The unique *Copper Scroll* is engraved on copper-based metal and records deposits of an enormous treasure in and around Jerusalem. Photograph courtesy of Bruce and Kenneth Zuckerman of West Semitic Research.

scripts. Because of the enormous amount of treasure in-volved—perhaps as much as several dozen tons buried in loca-tions in and around Jerusalem—many people are convinced that the treasures described in the document are fictional. Others, however, have argued that the list records the deposit of the treasures of the Jerusalem temple, perhaps tithes col-lected during the First Jewish Revolt (A.D. 66–74) that could not be taken to Jerusalem during the siege.[55]

The *Copper Scroll* begins with these words:

> At Horebbah which is in the Vale of Achor under the stairs which go eastwards forty cubits: a box (filled with) silver weighing in all seventeen talents. In the tomb of . . . the third: 100 gold bars. In the great cistern which is in the courtyard of the little colonnade, at its very bottom, closed with sediment towards the upper opening: nine hundred talents. At the hill of Kohlit, containers, sandalwood and ephods (priestly garments). The total of the offering and of the treasure: seven (talents?) and second tithe rendered un-clean. At the exit of the canal on the northern side, six cubits towards the cavity of immersion. In the hole of the water-proofed refuge, in going down towards the left, three cubits above the bottom: forty talents of silver.

The scroll continues with similar descriptions of hidden treasures. A few treasure seekers have exerted great efforts to discover the treasures described in this scroll, but with no success.

53. What are the *New Jerusalem* texts?

Several fragmented Hebrew and Aramaic documents pro-vide details regarding the New Jerusalem (i.e., the holy city that will be rebuilt in the last days to replace the old city of Jerusalem, distinct from its counterpart to be built by the Latter-day

Saints in Jackson County, Missouri). Because the documents were discovered in Caves 1, 2, 4, 5, and 11, they likely once formed a significant part of the Qumran library.

The texts describe a visionary or prophet who is led by a heavenly ministrant who shows him the dimensions and various parts of the New Jerusalem, including the gates, streets, houses, doors, thresholds, lintels, and stairs. One of the fragments reads in part, "And he measu[red from] this [ga]te to the eastern corner 25 stadia. *vacat* [empty space in the manuscript] And he led me into the city, and he measured each block of houses for its length and width, fifty-one reeds by fifty-one, in a square" (*New Jerusalem* 2:10–12). At times the ministrant describes various parts of the New Jerusalem, for example, "all [the streets of the city] are paved with white stone . . . marble and jasper" (1:7–9).

The literary form of the *New Jerusalem* texts recalls Ezekiel 40–46, in which Ezekiel was hosted by an angel who revealed to him the future Jerusalem temple and its dimensions.

54. What is the document called *Some Observances of the Law?*

Cave 4 yielded six tattered copies of a legal document called *Some Observances of the Law (4QMMT)*. It was written by a leader of the Qumran community, possibly the Teacher of Righteousness, and perhaps was addressed to that leader's opponents. The document sets forth many religious laws and precepts belonging to the Qumran community, including items regarding the religious calendar, practices relating to the temple and its sacrifices, laws about marriage and intermarriage, and rules pertaining to entry into the community.

Other topics addressed in the document include a discussion or mention of the offering of sacrifices from the Gentiles, bringing certain animal skins to the temple, purity laws regarding making vessels from the bones or skins of unclean animals, Jerusalem as the chosen place, sacrificing pregnant animals, eating unborn animals, items concerning the blind and the deaf, a prohibition against bringing dogs into Jerusalem, tithes and fruits given to the priests, and items concerning lepers.

The document concludes with the admonition "Understand all these (matters) and ask Him (God) to straighten your counsel and put you far away from thoughts of evil and the counsel of Belial" (*Some Observances of the Law* 3:5–6).

55. What is the *War Scroll*?

The *War Scroll* describes a war in the final age of the earth's history. In this war between the forces of good and evil, the wicked will be completely destroyed, ushering in an era of peace. The writers of the Dead Sea Scrolls, who believed that they were the true, restored Israel, compose the righteous army. The *War Scroll* begins by designating the righteous as "the sons of light," who are also described as "the children of Levi, Judah, and Benjamin." They are opposed by the "sons of darkness," identified as Edomites, Moabites, Ammonites, Philistines, the Kittim (the meaning of *Kittim* is unknown), and the "transgressors of the covenant." In the Old Testament the Edomites, Moabites, Ammonites, and the Philistines are enemies of Israel. The "transgressors of the covenant" are most likely mainstream Jews of the period who would not accept the views of the Dead Sea Scrolls writers, who believed that other Jews were living in a state of apostasy or were violating the law of Moses.

The *War Scroll* describes the organization of the army of Israel in detail and prescribes prayers, hymns, and exhortations to be spoken by the priests and Levites in the course of war.

Angelic beings, both good and evil, will also take part in the conflict. Ultimately it is God who will give victory to the righteous and who will usher in a golden age of light for the faithful. Interestingly, the *War Scroll* appears to be modeled on Roman military manuals, and the deployment of the army of God follows in some measure Roman patterns of warfare.

The *War Scroll* describes a future struggle between the "sons of darkness" and the righteous "sons of light," who will emerge victorious with God's help. Photograph courtesy of Ancient Biblical Manuscript Center, with permission from the Israel Antiquities Authority.

56. What is the *Temple Scroll?*

At over twenty-eight feet in length, the *Temple Scroll* is the longest of the scrolls discovered in the eleven Qumran caves. Scholars cannot agree on a more precise date for the scroll's composition than sometime between 150 B.C. and A.D. 1., nor are they certain of its author. Israeli scholar Yigael Yadin published an English translation of the scroll in 1977, along with photographs and commentary.

The *Temple Scroll* details the Qumran community's view of their temple of the last days. Photograph courtesy of Ancient Biblical Manuscript Center, with permission from the Israel Antiquities Authority.

The *Temple Scroll* examines various aspects of the temple complex, construction, and functions; it describes and provides the measurements of the sanctuary and its holy of holies, chambers and colonnades, mercy seat, cherubim, veil, table, golden lamp, altar, and courtyards. The architecture and structure of this temple is very different from Solomon's temple and the temple described in Ezekiel 40–46, for the *Temple Scroll* describes three concentric courts, each square in shape. The four gates of the inner court represent the four groups of the tribe of Levi. The middle court encompasses the inner court and features three gates on each of the four sides, twelve gates total, each one representing one of the tribes of Israel. The outer court encompasses the other courts and also has twelve gates.

The three courts were designed to inform temple officiators, workers, and worshippers of hierarchical sanctity—the innermost zone of the temple was the most sacred, and as one moved outward from that area the zones (and the respective ordinances or rituals performed therein) decreased in relative sanctity. Thus the temple building itself was the most holy place, the inner courtyard was next in holiness, and so on.

The *Temple Scroll* goes beyond the physical features of the temple to describe the ideal temple society and its covenant with God. The scroll describes sacrifices, purity regulations,

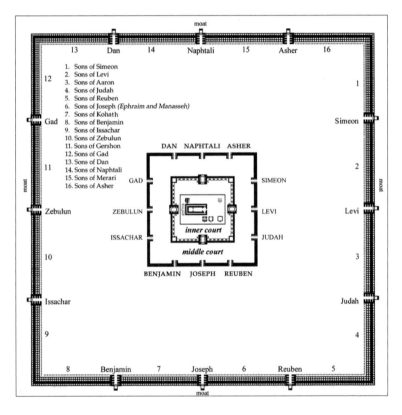

The *Temple Scroll* describes the Qumran community's view of the temple that they anticipated would be built at the end of times. Diagram by Jessica Taylor adapted from Yigael Yadin, *The Temple Scroll: The Hidden Law of the Dead Sea Sect,* 1985.

and judges and officers affiliated with the temple. It outlines laws relating to idolatry and apostasy, vows and oaths, priests, Levites, priestly dues, witnesses, sacrificial animals, conduct during war, rebellious sons, and crimes punishable by hanging. Many of the laws in this text pertain to the ritual purity or defilement of women.

The temple was to serve as a reminder of the awesome presence of God and the purity necessary to approach him. The future temple was to preserve a stricter ritual purity among the people, for the laws governing its sanctity were more restrictive than those pertaining to other Israelite temples, thereby lifting the level of the entire community to a higher state of purity.

57. What are the *Thanksgiving Hymns?*

The *Thanksgiving Hymns* scroll, discovered in Cave 1, was copied originally on two scrolls that were eventually sewn together into one scroll containing at least twenty-five hymns. The hymnbook-like collection of hymns is called *Thanksgiving Hymns* because of the frequent repetition of the phrase "I thank thee, O Lord." The hymns, which contain phraseology similar to the biblical psalms, include praises of God's judgments, his works of creation, and his acts of salvation. They describe the human condition and the tendency to sin. Like many of the biblical psalms, these hymns emphasize God's righteousness, mercy, and truth. The following selection from the *Thanksgiving Hymns* is representative sample.

Hymn 5

[I thank] Thee, O Lord,
    as befits the greatness of Thy power
    and the multitude of Thy marvels for ever and ever.
[Thou art a merciful God] and rich in [favours],

pardoning those who repent of their sin
and visiting the iniquity of the wicked.
[Thou delightest in] the free-will offering [of the righteous]
but iniquity Thou hatest always.
Thou hast favoured me, Thy servant,
with a spirit of knowledge,
[that I may choose] truth [and goodness]
and loathe all the ways of iniquity.
And I have loved Thee freely
and with all my heart;
[contemplating the mysteries of] Thy wisdom
[I have sought Thee].
For this is from Thy hand
and [nothing is] without [Thy will].

PART VIII

SPECIFIC INSIGHTS INTO
THE DEAD SEA SCROLLS

58. Do the scrolls contain previously unknown religious writings?

Many of the writings represented among the Dead Sea Scrolls were unknown before the scrolls' discovery in the years 1947 through 1956. These writings include legal texts *(Temple Scroll, Community Rule, Some Observances of the Law [4QMMT])*, hymns and poems *(Thanksgiving Hymns, Apocryphal Psalms, Noncanonical Psalms)*, calendrical texts *(Phases of the Moon, Calendars of Priestly Courses, Zodiacal Calendar with a Brontologion)*, biblical commentaries *(Commentary on Micah, Commentary on Habakkuk, Commentary on Psalms)*, apocryphal works *(Prayer of Enosh and Enoch, Elisha Apocryphon, Joshua Apocryphon)*, biblically related or based works *(New Jerusalem, Prayer of Nabonidus, Words of Moses, Book of Noah, Ages of the Creation)*, prayers and liturgical works *(Liturgical Work, Purification Ritual, Blessings, Benedictions, Prayers for Festivals)*, and other miscellaneous texts.

These texts provide significant information regarding the

Hebrew and Aramaic languages, how some Jews worshipped during the centuries before the destruction of the Jerusalem temple, and the religious views of the Jews of the Qumran community.

59. Is the plan of salvation attested in the scrolls?

Responding to this same question, Brigham Young University professor Dana M. Pike discussed possible parallels between Latter-day Saint doctrine concerning the plan of salvation and the beliefs set forth in the nonbiblical scrolls. Pike cautiously concludes that a "clear or comprehensive understanding of this plan is not evidenced at Qumran." Continuing, he notes: "Though there are concepts that I have described as corrupted echoes of true doctrines, there are simply too many key points of the plan of salvation absent from the preserved texts. Doctrines such as the fall, the infinite atonement of the Savior, clear indications of a universal, physical resurrection, and eternal ordinances requiring the holy Melchizedek Priesthood are not attested." Pike adds that the scrolls "cannot teach Latter-day Saints anything about the plan of salvation that has not already been revealed by the Lord through his authorized servants."[56]

60. Do the scrolls mention premortal life?

The scrolls do not speak of premortal life, although it is possible to see "corrupted echoes" in them because the people who lived at Qumran were "heirs to the prophetic legacy that is partially preserved in the Hebrew Bible (the Christian Old Testament)."[57] Dana M. Pike further observes that "the Qumran sectarian scrolls indicate that God created all things, including good and evil spirits, as well as the spirits or souls of people before they existed in the flesh, and that God determined which people would be saved and which people would be destroyed. These passages suggest . . . corrupted echoes of the war in heaven and of God's foreordination of his spirit children, concepts that Latter-day Saints believe were known and understood in previous gospel dispensations. However, by the time of the Qumran community it appears that their understanding was well off the track of true doctrine."[58]

61. What were the community's hymns of praise?

Several scrolls contained hymns used by the Qumran community during daily worship and annual festivals. One scroll comprises forty-nine psalms, forty-one of which are the same as those in our biblical book of Psalms (the remaining eight psalms are apocryphal). According to this scroll, King David composed a great number of psalms and songs:

> YHWH [Jehovah] gave [David] an intelligent and brilliant spirit, and he wrote 3,600 psalms and 364 songs to sing before the altar for the daily perpetual sacrifice, for all the days of the year; and 52 songs of the Sabbath offerings; and 30 songs for the New Moons, for Feast-days and for the Day of Atonement.
>
> In all, the songs which he uttered were 446, and 4 songs to make music on behalf of those stricken (by evil spirits).
>
> In all, they were 4,050.
>
> All these he uttered through prophecy which was given him from before the Most High.
>
> (*An Account of David's Poems*)

In addition to these psalms, the Dead Sea Scrolls include thirty nonbiblical hymns that are called the *Thanksgiving Hymns* (see question 57). Brigham Young University professor David Rolph Seely explains that "five of these are part of *Barki Nafshi*—a single text of hymns blessing the Lord, named after the opening phrase 'Bless, O My Soul.'"[59] Seely translates a portion of one of the hymns as follows:

Bless, O my soul, the Lord,
> for all his wonders forever,
> and blessed be his name.
For he has delivered the soul of the poor
> and the humble he has not despised,
> and he has not forgotten the distress of the helpless.
He has opened his eyes to the helpless,
> and the cry of the orphans he has heard,
> and he has turned his ears to their cry.
In the abundance of his mercy he was gracious to the needy
> and he has opened their eyes to see his ways
> and their ears to hear his teaching.
And he circumcised the foreskin of their heart
> and he delivered them because of his grace
> and he set their feet to the way.[60]

In this hymn the Lord is praised because he has "delivered [the unfortunate] because of his grace."

62. What was the Qumran community's attitude toward prayer?

Similar to other Jewish groups of the period, the Qumran community prayed regularly. According to David Rolph Seely, "Prayer could be offered at any time, in any place, in any circumstance, and at Qumran there were also set times for regular prayer in the morning and in the evening. The *Community Rule* specifies prayer when the light of day first appears in the morning and when it disappears in the evening."[61]

A hymn located at the end of the *Community Rule* describes the beautiful attitude that the Qumran community held toward prayer:

When I stretch out hand and foot I will praise his name.
When I go out and come in, sit and rise, and when laid on
my couch, I will cry for joy to him. I will praise him with the
offering of the utterance of my lips in the row of men, and
before I lift my hand to enjoy the delights of the world's pro-
duce. In the beginning of terror and dread, and in the abode
of affliction and distress I will bless him for (his) exceed-
ingly wondrous activity. I will meditate upon his power, and
upon his mercies I will lean all day.[62]

63. Were any business records discovered among the scrolls?

A few of the scroll fragments are business records of one
type or another. These documents pertain to land sales, debt,
money, grain, personal property, and related items.[63]

64. What about the name Alma, discovered in one of the Bar Kokhba texts?

In the years 1960 and 1961 Israeli archaeologist Yigael
Yadin excavated a cave in a wadi known as Nahal Hever, located west of the Dead Sea at a point north of Masada and
south of Qumran. Properly speaking, the cave does not belong
to the group of caves near Qumran where the Dead Sea Scrolls
were discovered. Yadin and his team discovered a number of
significant artifacts, including one pair of women's sandals,
kitchen knives, wooden bowls, cooking pots, a mirror, pieces
of clothing, and a jewelry box. The cave also yielded a bundle
of more than forty papyrus documents bound in rags and tied
with palm-frond strings.

The documents comprised letters and deeds belonging to
the leader of the Second Jewish Revolt (A.D. 132–35), Shimeon
bar Kosiba (or Simeon Bar Kokhba). Among the documents
was land-lease agreement written in Hebrew and containing

the name Alma. The papyrus sheet consists of twenty-six lines
and about two hundred words. Part of the text reads as follows:

> Of their own free will, on this day, have Eleazar son of
> Eleazar son of Hitta and Eliezer son of Samuel, both of En-
> gedi, and Tehinnah son of Simeon and Alma son of Judah

The name Alma, boxed and enlarged here, appears in one of the scrolls
found in the Cave of the Letters, in Nahal Hever. Written in Hebrew, this
business document dates to A.D. 134. Photograph courtesy of David W.
Hawkinson.

both of ha-Luhith in the (coastal) district of Agaltain, now
resident in En-gedi, wished to divide up amongst themselves the places that they have leased from Jonathan son of
MHNYM the administrator of Simeon ben Kosiba, Prince
of Israel, at En-gedi.[64]

The so-called Alma deed is significant for Latter-day Saints
because it reveals that the name Alma did in fact exist as a male
name in antiquity just decades after the mortal ministry of
Jesus Christ.

65. What is known about Enoch in the scrolls?

Hugh W. Nibley, a professor emeritus of history and religion at Brigham Young University, has observed that "aside
from brief genealogical notes, all that the Bible tells us about
Enoch is that 'he walked with God, and was not' (Genesis 5:25),
and that he prophesied the coming of the Lord to execute judgment (Jude 1:14)."[65] Though sparsely represented in the Bible,
Enoch is "the colossus who bestrides the Apocrypha as no
other,"[66] a figure of "extraordinary strength and pervasiveness."[67]

Enoch is also found widely in the Dead Sea Scrolls texts of
1 Enoch, Jubilees, and the Aramaic *Genesis Apocryphon,* reveal-
ing him to be a mighty prophet with special gifts. According to
these texts, he was a great writer, "the first among men that are
born on earth who learned writing and knowledge and wisdom" (*Jubilees* 4:17). He was granted access to divine books
and great knowledge, and he "observed the heavenly tablet, and
read them carefully, and read the book of all the deeds of
mankind to the remotest generations" (*1 Enoch* 81:1, 2).

The Dead Sea Scrolls identify Enoch as an astronomer. The
book of *1 Enoch* is referred to as Enoch's "Astronomical Book,"
or "the book of the courses of the luminaries of the heavens"
(*1 Enoch* 72:1). One scholar believes that the sources attribute

"the solar calendar of 364 days . . . to Enoch, the original astronomer."[68]

While the scrolls add much to the scanty information about Enoch in the Bible (see Genesis 5), the account of Enoch in the Latter-day Saints' Pearl of Great Price comprises the most complete and accurate record of this great prophet.

Nibley also observes that "in giving us a much fuller account than the Bible of how the flood came about, the Book of Enoch settles the moral issue with several telling parts: (1) God's reluctance to send the Flood and his great sorrow at the event. (2) The peculiar brand of wickedness that made the Flood mandatory. (3) The frank challenge of the wicked to have God do His worst."[69] The Dead Sea Scrolls record many of the people's iniquities as well as God's weeping over the necessity of destroying his own creation.

There is a further note of interest. In the Book of Moses account in the Pearl of Great Price, there appears "out of the blue . . . the name of the only nonbiblical individual named in the whole book—Mahijah (Moses 6:40)."[70] Strikingly, the name Mahujah (MHWY—"the semi-vowels *w* and *y* are written very much alike in the Aramaic script and are sometimes confused by scribes"[71]) also appears in the Enoch materials in the Dead Sea Scrolls. Moses 6:40 reads: "There came a man unto him, whose name was Mahijah, and said unto him: Tell us plainly who thou art, and from whence thou comest?" This is strikingly similar to *4QEnoch Giants* 1:20: "And they summoned MHWY and he came to them: And they asked him and sent him to Enoch."

66. Are the names Zenos or Zenock found in the scrolls?

Neither Zenos nor Zenock is mentioned in the scrolls. However, the name Mahujah is found in the Enoch fragments (see question 65), and the name Alma is found on a document found in a cave in Nahal Hever (see question 64).

67. What may be learned about Judaism from the scrolls?

The scrolls, more than any other archaeological find, have increased our awareness of the Essenes, a group of Jews whose practices and beliefs differed from those of other Jewish groups active in the first two centuries B.C. and the first century A.D.

Besides illuminating the rich variety of Judaism in antiquity, the scrolls permit us to see one group of Jews who took a more comprehensive and embracing view of scripture (because their writings "are unaffected by either Christian or rabbinic censorship")[72] and who took a more exacting view of the observance of festivals and sacrificial practices and of community leadership inspired by the Holy Spirit.

68. Do the scrolls refer to Joseph Smith or other latter-day figures?

The Qumran writings make no references, explicit or implicit, to Joseph Smith or other latter-day religious or historical figures.

69. Has the LDS Church taken a position on the scrolls?

General Authorities of the Church of Jesus Christ of Latter-day Saints have never taken an official position or made an official statement on the Dead Sea Scrolls with regard to their discovery or content. Although a few Latter-day Saint scholars have done extensive work on the scrolls and have occasionally published their findings in periodicals of the LDS Church, such as the *Improvement Era, Church News,* and *Ensign,* these findings represent the opinions of individual scholars and are not to be considered as representing the LDS Church's position on any given topic.

70. Where can I learn more about the scrolls?

We have prepared a suggested reading list of articles and books on the Dead Sea Scrolls. The list includes studies by Latter-day Saint scholars, English translations of the scrolls, and general studies.

STUDIES BY LATTER-DAY SAINT SCHOLARS

Bradford, Gerald M., ed. *Ancient Scrolls from the Dead Sea: Photographs and Commentary on a Unique Collection of Scrolls.* Provo, Utah: FARMS, 1997.

Brown, S. Kent. "The Dead Sea Scrolls: A Mormon Perspective." *BYU Studies* 23 (winter 1983): 49–66.

Cloward, Robert A. "Dead Sea Scrolls: LDS Perspective." In *Encyclopedia of Mormonism,* edited by Daniel H. Ludlow, 1:363–64. New York: Macmillan, 1992.

Nibley, Hugh W. "Apocryphal Writings and Teachings of the Dead Sea Scrolls." In *Temple and Cosmos.* The Collected Works of Hugh Nibley, vol. 12. Salt Lake City: Deseret Book and FARMS, 1992.

———. "Churches in the Wilderness." In *Nibley on the Timely and the Timeless.* Provo, Utah: BYU Religious Studies Center, 1978. Reprinted in *The Prophetic Book of Mormon.* Salt Lake City: Deseret Book and FARMS, 1989.

———. "The Dead Sea Scrolls and the Book of Mormon." In *An Approach to the Book of Mormon,* 3rd ed. The Collected Works of Hugh Nibley, vol. 6. Salt Lake City: Deseret Book and FARMS, 1988.

———. "The Dead Sea Scrolls: Some Questions and Answers." *Instructor,* July 1963, 233–35. Reprinted in *Old Testament and Related Studies.* The Collected Works of Hugh Nibley, vol. 1. Salt Lake City: Deseret Book and FARMS, 1986.

———. "Appendix 1: From the Dead Sea Scrolls." In *The*

Message of the Joseph Smith Papyri. Salt Lake City: Deseret Book, 1975.

———. "More Voices from the Dust." *Instructor,* March 1956, 71–72, 74. Reprinted in *Old Testament and Related Studies.* The Collected Works of Hugh Nibley, vol. 1. Salt Lake City: Deseret Book and FARMS, 1986.

———. "Qumran and the Companions of the Cave." *Revue de Qumran* 5 (April 1965): 177–98. Reprinted as "Qumran and the Companions of the Cave: The Haunted Wilderness." In *Old Testament and Related Studies.* The Collected Works of Hugh Nibley, vol. 1. Salt Lake City: Deseret Book and FARMS, 1986.

———. *Since Cumorah.* 2nd ed. The Collected Works of Hugh Nibley, vol. 7. Salt Lake City: Deseret Book and FARMS, 1988.

Parry, Donald W. "The Contribution of the Dead Sea Scrolls to Biblical Understanding." In *LDS Perspectives on the Dead Sea Scrolls,* edited by Donald W. Parry and Dana M. Pike. Provo, Utah: FARMS, 1997.

———. "4QSam[a] and the Tetragrammaton." In *Current Research and Technological Developments on the Dead Sea Scrolls: Conference on the Texts from the Judean Desert, Jerusalem, 30 April 1995,* edited by Donald W. Parry and Stephen D. Ricks. Leiden: E. J. Brill, 1996.

———. "Retelling Samuel: Echoes of the Books of Samuel in the Dead Sea Scrolls." *Revue de Qumran* 17 (1996): 293–306.

Parry, Donald W., and Steven W. Booras. "The Dead Sea Scrolls CD-ROM Database Project." In *Current Research and Technological Developments on the Dead Sea Scrolls: Conference on the Texts from the Judean Desert, Jerusalem, 30 April 1995,* edited by Donald W. Parry and Stephen D. Ricks. Leiden: E. J. Brill, 1996.

Parry, Donald W., Steven W. Booras, and E. Jan Wilson. "The FARMS-BYU Dead Sea Scrolls Electronic Database," in *LDS Perspectives on the Dead Sea Scrolls,* edited by Donald W. Parry and Dana M. Pike. Provo, Utah: FARMS, 1997.

Parry, Donald W., and Dana M. Pike, eds. *LDS Perspectives on the Dead Sea Scrolls.* Provo, Utah: FARMS, 1997.

Pike, Dana M. "The Book of Numbers at Qumran: Texts and Context." In *Current Research and Technological Developments on the Dead Sea Scrolls: Conference on the Texts from the Judean Desert, Jerusalem, 30 April 1995,* edited by Donald W. Parry and Stephen D. Ricks. Leiden: E. J. Brill, 1996.

———. "Is the Plan of Salvation Attested in the Dead Sea Scrolls?" In *LDS Perspectives on the Dead Sea Scrolls,* edited by Donald W. Parry and Dana M. Pike. Provo, Utah: FARMS, 1997.

———. "The 'Congregation of YHWH' in the Bible and at Qumran." *Revue de Qumran* 17 (1996): 233–40.

Ricks, Stephen D. "The Book of Mormon and the Dead Sea Scrolls." In *LDS Perspectives on the Dead Sea Scrolls,* edited by Donald W. Parry and Dana M. Pike. Provo, Utah: FARMS, 1997.

———. "Who Wrote the Dead Sea Scrolls?" Provo, Utah: FARMS, 1993.

Rogers, Lewis M. "The Dead Sea Scrolls: Qumran Calmly Revisited." *BYU Studies* 2/2 (1960): 109–28.

Seely, David R. "The *Barki Nafshi* Texts (4Q434–439)." In *Current Research and Technological Developments on the Dead Sea Scrolls: Conference on the Texts from the Judean Desert, Jerusalem, 30 April 1995,* edited by Donald W. Parry and Stephen D. Ricks. Leiden: E. J. Brill, 1996.

———. "The 'Circumcised Heart' in 4Q434 *Barki Nafshi*." *Revue de Qumran* 17 (1996): 527–35.

————. "Praise, Prayer, and Worship at Qumran." In *LDS Perspectives on the Dead Sea Scrolls,* edited by Donald W. Parry and Dana M. Pike. Provo, Utah: FARMS, 1997.

Skinner, Andrew C. "The Ancient People of Qumran: An Introduction to the Dead Sea Scrolls." In *LDS Perspectives on the Dead Sea Scrolls,* edited by Donald W. Parry and Dana M. Pike. Provo, Utah: FARMS, 1997.

Tvedtnes, John A. "The Dead Sea Scrolls." In *The Church of the Old Testament,* 2nd ed. Salt Lake City: Deseret Book, 1980.

Woodward, Scott R. "Putting the Pieces Together: DNA and the Dead Sea Scrolls." In *LDS Perspectives on the Dead Sea Scrolls,* edited by Donald W. Parry and Dana M. Pike. Provo, Utah: FARMS, 1997.

Woodward, Scott R., Gila Kahila, Patricia Smith, Charles Greenblatt, Joe Zias, and Magen Broshi. "Analysis of Parchment Fragments from the Judean Desert Using DNA Techniques." In *Current Research and Technological Developments on the Dead Sea Scrolls: Conference on the Texts from the Judean Desert, Jerusalem, 30 April 1995,* edited by Donald W. Parry and Stephen D. Ricks. Leiden: E. J. Brill, 1996.

ENGLISH TRANSLATIONS

García Martínez, Florentino, trans. *The Dead Sea Scrolls Translated: The Qumran Texts in English.* Translated into English by Wilfred G. E. Watson. Leiden: E. J. Brill, 1994.

Vermes, Geza. *The Complete Dead Sea Scrolls in English.* New York: Penguin, 1997.

Wise, Michael, Martin Abegg Jr., and Edward Cook. *The Dead Sea Scrolls: A New Translation.* San Francisco: Harper, 1996.

GENERAL STUDIES

Collins, John J. *The Scepter and the Star: The Messiahs of the Dead Sea Scrolls and Other Ancient Literature.* New York: Doubleday, 1995.

Cross, Frank Moore. *The Ancient Library of Qumran.* 3rd ed. Minneapolis: Fortress, 1995.

Fitzmyer, Joseph A. *Responses to 101 Questions on the Dead Sea Scrolls.* New York: Paulist, 1992.

García Martínez, Florentino, and Donald W. Parry, eds. *A Bibliography of the Finds in the Desert of Judah, 1970–95.* Leiden: E. J. Brill, 1996.

García Martínez, Florentino, and Julio Trebolle Barrera. *The People of the Dead Sea Scrolls: Their Writings, Beliefs and Practices.* Leiden: E. J. Brill, 1993.

Ringgren, Helmer. *The Faith of Qumran: Theology of the Dead Sea Scrolls.* New York: Crossroads, 1995.

Scanlin, Harold. *The Dead Sea Scrolls and Modern Translations of the Old Testament.* Wheaton, Ill.: Tyndale House, 1993.

Schiffman, Lawrence H. *Reclaiming the Dead Sea Scrolls.* Philadelphia: Jewish Publication Society, 1994.

VanderKam, James C. *The Dead Sea Scrolls Today.* Grand Rapids, Mich.: Eerdmans, 1994.

Yadin, Yigael. *The Scroll of the War of the Sons of Light against the Sons of Darkness.* London: Oxford University Press, 1962.

———. *The Temple Scroll: The Hidden Law of the Dead Sea Sect.* New York: Random House, 1985.

NOTES

1. Joseph A. Fitzmyer, *Responses to 101 Questions on the Dead Sea Scrolls* (New York: Paulist Press, 1992).

2. Stephen Pfann mentioned this in a personal conversation with Stephen Ricks, 31 May 1993.

3. Geza Vermes, *The Dead Sea Scrolls in English,* 3rd ed. (London: Penguin, 1987), xiii.

4. Hans Wehr, *A Dictionary of Modern Written Arabic,* ed. J Milton Cowan, 3rd ed. (Ithaca: Spoken Language Services, 1976), 231, 1059; compare Fitzmyer, *101 Questions,* 2.

5. See Philip R. Davies, *Qumran* (Grand Rapids, Mich.: Eerdmans, 1982), 30.

6. See ibid., 44–48.

7. See ibid.

8. See LDS Bible Dictionary, s.v. "Apocrypha," for a discussion of these and other apocryphal books.

9. See, for example, James C. VanderKam, *The Dead Sea Scrolls Today* (Grand Rapids, Mich.: Eerdmans, 1994), 93–95; and Hershel Shanks, ed., *Understanding the Dead Sea Scrolls: A Reader from the Biblical Archeology Review* (New York: Random House, 1992), 35–84.

10. See Todd S. Beall, *Josephus' Description of the Essenes Illustrated by the Dead Sea Scrolls* (New York: Cambridge University Press, 1988).

11. See Josephus, *Jewish Wars* 2.8.2 (paragraph 119), 2.8.3 (122, 123), 2.8.4 (126), 2.8.9 (147).

12. Beall, *Josephus' Description of the Essenes*, 15.

13. Pliny the Elder, *Natural History* 5.17; see H. Rackham's English translation in the Loeb Classical Library edition of Pliny's work (Cambridge: Harvard University Press, 1969).

14. See Frank Moore Cross, "The Development of the Jewish Scripts," in *The Bible and the Ancient Near East: Essays in Honor of William Foxwell Albright*, ed. G. Ernest Wright (Garden City: Anchor Books, 1965), 136.

15. See the chart in Lawrence H. Schiffman, *Reclaiming the Dead Sea Scrolls* (Philadelphia: Jewish Publication Society, 1994), 32–33.

16. Schiffman, *Reclaiming the Dead Sea Scrolls*, xxi.

17. Their excavations are summarized in "How and Where Did the Qumranites Live?" in *The Provo International Conference on the Dead Sea Scrolls: Technological Innovations, New Texts, and Reformulated Issues*, ed. Donald W. Parry and Eugene Ulrich (Leiden: E. J. Brill, 1999), 266–73.

18. Frank Moore Cross, *Ancient Library of Qumran*, 3rd ed. (Minneapolis: Fortress, 1995) 39–40.

19. See Davies, *Qumran*, 44–48.

20. See David E. Aune, *Prophecy in Early Christianity and the Ancient Mediterranean World* (Grand Rapids, Mich.: Eerdmans, 1983), 342–43.

21. See Florentino García Martínez and Julio Trebolle Barrera, *The People of the Dead Sea Scrolls: Their Writings, Beliefs and Practices* (Leiden: E. J. Brill, 1995), 73, 90.

22. Ibid., 80, 88.

23. Frank Moore Cross, "The Scrolls and the New Testament," *Christian Century* 72 (August 1955): 970; compare Cross, "Dead Sea Scrolls: Overview," in *Encyclopedia of Mormonism*, ed. Daniel H. Ludlow (New York: Macmillan, 1992), 1:462, in which Cross describes the writers of the Dead Sea Scrolls as a "church of anticipation."

24. Schiffman, *Reclaiming the Dead Sea Scrolls*, 331.

25. Zadokites were descendants of the priest Zadok, who served

in the high priesthood during most of the First and Second Temple periods.

26. See the chronological table in the LDS Bible Dictionary, 641.

27. Millar Burrows, *Burrows on the Dead Sea Scrolls* (Grand Rapids, Mich.: Baker, 1978), 328.

28. Schiffman, *Reclaiming the Dead Sea Scrolls,* 103; see G. R. Beasley-Murray, *Baptism in the New Testament* (Grand Rapids, Mich.: Eerdmans, 1973), 11–18.

29. Schiffman, *Reclaiming the Dead Sea Scrolls,* 103.

30. Cross, *Ancient Library of Qumran,* 40.

31. See Schiffman, *Reclaiming the Dead Sea Scrolls,* 11.

32. Geza Vermes, "The War over the Scrolls," *New York Review of Books,* 11 August 1994, 10.

33. García Martínez and Barrera, *People of the Dead Sea Scrolls,* 194.

34. Scott R. Woodward et al., "Analysis of Parchment Fragments from the Judean Desert Using DNA Techniques," in *Current Research and Technological Developments on the Dead Sea Scrolls: Conference on the Texts from the Judean Desert, Jerusalem, 30 April 1995,* ed. Donald W. Parry and Stephen D. Ricks (Leiden: E. J. Brill, 1996), 216.

35. See VanderKam, *Dead Sea Scrolls Today,* 30.

36. See Martin Abegg Jr., Peter Flint, and Eugene Ulrich, "Why Is Esther Missing from Qumran?" *Bible Review,* August 1999, 2.

37. John Tvedtnes, "The Isaiah Variants in the Book of Mormon" (Provo, Utah: FARMS, 1981).

38. See VanderKam, *Dead Sea Scrolls Today,* 142–44, 149, 157.

39. See Harold Scanlin, *The Dead Sea Scrolls and Modern Translations of the Old Testament* (Wheaton, Ill.: Tyndale House, 1993), 26.

40. See ibid., 34.

41. Ibid., 27.

42. The two versions are the Samaritan Pentateuch and the Masoretic Text. See VanderKam, *Dead Sea Scrolls Today,* 125.

43. The material in this section has been adapted from Donald W. Parry, "The Contribution of the Dead Sea Scrolls to Biblical Understanding," in *LDS Perspectives on the Dead Sea Scrolls,* ed. Donald W. Parry and Dana M. Pike (Provo, Utah: FARMS, 1997), 59–60.

44. For a complete discussion of this missing verse of scripture, see Frank Moore Cross, "The Ammonite Oppression of the Tribes of Gad and Reuben: Missing Verses from 1 Samuel 11 Found in 4QSamuel[a]," in *History, Historiography and Interpretation: Studies in Biblical and Cuneiform Literatures,* ed. H. Tadmor and M. Weinfeld (Jerusalem: Magnes, 1983), 148–58; Emanuel Tov, *Textual Criticism of the Hebrew Bible* (Minneapolis: Fortress Press, 1992), 342–43.

45. Translation is by Donald W. Parry. Josephus refers to this incident of King Nahash in *Antiquities* 6.68–71.

46. David Rolph Seely, "Praise, Prayer, and Worship at Qumran," in *LDS Perspectives on the Dead Sea Scrolls,* ed. Parry and Pike, 98.

47. For a discussion of views regarding John the Baptist and Qumran, see García Martínez and Barrera, *People of the Dead Sea Scrolls,* 205–6.

48. See ibid., 214–15.

49. For a full discussion on parallels between the Qumran texts and the New Testament, see García Martínez and Barrera, *People of the Dead Sea Scrolls,* 203–20.

50. Florentino García Martínez, *The Dead Sea Scrolls Translated: The Qumran Texts in English,* trans. Wilfred G. E. Watson, 2nd ed. (Leiden: E. J. Brill, 1994), 200.

51. See VanderKam, *Dead Sea Scrolls Today,* 56–57; García Martínez and Barrera, *People of the Dead Sea Scrolls,* 52–53; Geza Vermes, *The Complete Dead Sea Scrolls in English* (London: Penguin, 1997), 113–14; Michael A. Knibb, *The Qumran Community* (Cambridge: Cambridge University Press, 1987), 13–15.

52. See Moshe Weinfeld, *The Organizational Pattern and the Penal Code of the Qumran Sect: A Comparison with Guilds and Religious Associations of the Hellenistic-Roman Period* (Fribourg: Vandenhoeck and Ruprecht, 1986), 21–23, 43–44, 48–55, 58–73, 78–79.

53. Vermes, *Complete Dead Sea Scrolls in English,* 100.

54. An earlier, bootlegged edition was published by John M. Allegro, *The Treasure of the Copper Scroll: The Opening and Decipherment of the Most Mysterious of the Dead Sea Scrolls, A Unique Inventory of Buried Treasure* (New York: Doubleday, 1960).

55. See Vermes, *Complete Dead Sea Scrolls in English*, 583–84; Shanks, *Understanding the Dead Sea Scrolls*, 227–41.

56. Dana M. Pike, "Is the Plan of Salvation Attested in the Dead Sea Scrolls?" in *LDS Perspectives on the Dead Sea Scrolls*, ed. Parry and Pike, 90.

57. Ibid., 75.

58. Ibid., 81.

59. Seely, "Praise, Prayer, and Worship at Qumran," 110.

60. Ibid.

61. Ibid., 100.

62. Translated by Elisha Qimron and James Charlesworth, quoted in Seely, "Praise, Prayer, and Worship at Qumran," 100.

63. See VanderKam, *Dead Sea Scrolls Today*, 69.

64. Yigael Yadin, "Expedition D—The Cave of the Letters," *Israel Exploration Journal* 12 (1962): 250.

65. Hugh W. Nibley, *Enoch the Prophet* (Salt Lake City: Deseret Book and FARMS, 1986), 56 n. 1.

66. Ibid., 19.

67. G. W. Anderson, "Enoch, Books of," in *Encyclopedia Britannica* (1973), 8:605, cited in Nibley, *Enoch the Prophet*, 56 n. 2.

68. James C. VanderKam, *Enoch and the Growth of the Apocalyptic Tradition* (Washington, D.C.: The Catholic Biblical Association of America, 1984), 90.

69. Nibley, *Enoch the Prophet*, 4.

70. Ibid., 277.

71. Ibid., 278.

72. Vermes, *Complete Dead Sea Scrolls in English*, 24.

THE FOUNDATION FOR ANCIENT RESEARCH AND MORMON STUDIES

The Foundation for Ancient Research and Mormon Studies (FARMS) encourages and supports research and publication about the Book of Mormon: Another Testament of Jesus Christ and other ancient scriptures.

FARMS is a nonprofit, tax-exempt educational foundation at Brigham Young University. Its main research interests in the scriptures include ancient history, language, literature, culture, geography, politics, religion, and law. Although research on such subjects is of secondary importance when compared with the spiritual and eternal messages of the scriptures, solid scholarly research can supply certain kinds of useful information, even if only tentatively, concerning many significant and interesting questions about the ancient backgrounds, origins, composition, and meanings of scripture.

The work of the Foundation rests on the premise that the Book of Mormon and other scriptures were written by prophets of God. Belief in this premise—in the divinity of scripture—is a matter of faith. Religious truths require divine witness to establish the faith of the believer. While scholarly research cannot replace that witness, such studies may reinforce and encourage individual testimonies by fostering understanding and appreciation of the scriptures. It is hoped that this information will help people to "come unto Christ" (Jacob 1:7) and to understand and take more seriously these ancient witnesses of the atonement of Jesus Christ, the Son of God.

The Foundation works to make interim and final reports about its research available widely, promptly, and economically, both in scholarly and in popular formats. FARMS publishes information about the Book of Mormon and other ancient scripture in the *Insights* newsletter, books and research papers, *FARMS Review of Books, Journal of Book of Mormon Studies,* reprints of published scholarly papers, and videos and audiotapes. FARMS also supports the preparation of the Collected Works of Hugh Nibley series.

To facilitate the sharing of information, FARMS sponsors lectures, seminars, symposia, firesides, and radio and television broadcasts in which research findings are communicated to working scholars and to anyone interested in faithful, reliable information about the scriptures. Through Research Press, a publishing arm of the Foundation, FARMS publishes materials addressed primarily to working scholars.

For more information about the Foundation and its activities, contact the FARMS office at 1-800-327-6715 or (801) 373-5111. You can also visit the FARMS Web site at http://farms.byu.edu.

FARMS Publications

Teachings of the Book of Mormon

The Geography of Book of Mormon Events: A Source Book

The Book of Mormon Text Reformatted according to Parallelistic Patterns

Eldin Ricks's Thorough Concordance of the LDS Standard Works

A Guide to Publications on the Book of Mormon: A Selected Annotated Bibliography

Book of Mormon Authorship Revisited: The Evidence for Ancient Origins

Ancient Scrolls from the Dead Sea: Photographs and Commentary on a Unique Collection of Scrolls

LDS Perspectives on the Dead Sea Scrolls

Isaiah in the Book of Mormon

King Benjamin's Speech: "That Ye May Learn Wisdom"

Mormons, Scripture, and the Ancient World: Studies in Honor of John L. Sorenson

Latter-day Christianity: Ten Basic Issues

Illuminating the Sermon at the Temple and Sermon on the Mount

Scripture Study: Tools and Suggestions

Finding Biblical Hebrew and Other Ancient Literary Forms in the Book of Mormon

Charting the Book of Mormon: Visual Aids for Personal Study and Teaching

Pressing Forward with the Book of Mormon: The FARMS Updates of the 1990s

King Benjamin's Speech Made Simple

Romans 1: Notes and Reflections

The Temple in Time and Eternity

Mormon's Map

Periodicals

Insights: A Window on the Ancient World

FARMS Review of Books

Journal of Book of Mormon Studies

Reprint Series

Book of Mormon Authorship: New Light on Ancient Origins

The Doctrine and Covenants by Themes

Offenders for a Word

Copublished with Deseret Book Company

An Ancient American Setting for the Book of Mormon

Warfare in the Book of Mormon

By Study and Also by Faith: Essays in Honor of Hugh W. Nibley

The Sermon at the Temple and the Sermon on the Mount

Rediscovering the Book of Mormon

Reexploring the Book of Mormon

Of All Things! Classic Quotations from Hugh Nibley

The Allegory of the Olive Tree

Temples of the Ancient World

Expressions of Faith: Testimonies from LDS Scholars

Feasting on the Word: The Literary Testimony of the Book of Mormon

The Collected Works of Hugh Nibley

Old Testament and Related Studies

Enoch the Prophet

The World and the Prophets

Mormonism and Early Christianity

Lehi in the Desert; The World of the Jaredites; There Were Jaredites

An Approach to the Book of Mormon

Since Cumorah

The Prophetic Book of Mormon

Approaching Zion

The Ancient State

Tinkling Cymbals and Sounding Brass

Temple and Cosmos

Brother Brigham Challenges the Saints

Published through Research Press

Pre-Columbian Contact with the Americas across the Oceans: An Annotated Bibliography

A Comprehensive Annotated Book of Mormon Bibliography

New World Figurine Project, vol. 1

Images of Ancient America: Visualizing Book of Mormon Life

Chiasmus in Antiquity (reprint)

Chiasmus Bibliography

Publications of the FARMS Center for the Preservation of Ancient Religious Texts

Dead Sea Scrolls Electronic Reference Library

The Incoherence of the Philosophers

The Niche of Lights

The Philosophy of Illumination